God-Centred Evangelism

A Presentation of the
Scriptural Theology of Evangelism

R. B. KUIPER

Kuiper, Rienk Bouke, 1886 –

The Banner of Truth Trust

Copyright 1961, by Baker Book House
First published 1961
First Banner of Truth Trust edition 1966
Reprinted 1978

ISBN 0 85151 110 4

THE BANNER OF TRUTH TRUST
3 Murrayfield Road, Edinburgh EH12 6EL
PO Box 621, Carlisle, Pennsylvania 17013, USA

Printed and bound in Great Britain by
Hazell Watson & Viney Ltd, Aylesbury, Bucks

To
My Wife
on the Golden Anniversary
of Our Wedding
1911 – June 18 – 1961

A DISTINCTION IS SOMETIMES MADE BETWEEN missions and evangelism, missions being conceived of as the bringing of the gospel to the unsaved at a distance, and evangelism being thought of as the bringing of the gospel to the unsaved who are near at hand. That restricted usage of the term *evangelism* is difficult to justify. Evangelism is simply the promulgation of the evangel. The conveying of the evangel to the antipodes is as deserving of the name *evangelism* as is the conveying of the evangel to one's next-door neighbours. In the title of this volume and throughout the volume *evangelism* is employed in the sense ascribed to it in *Evangelism for the World Today as Interpreted by Christian Leaders throughout the World*, a 1938 publication of the International Missionary Council; namely, the bringing of the gospel to the unsaved *anywhere*.

The following definition of *missions* is taken from J. H. Bavinck's recent study *An Introduction to the Science of Missions*: 'Missions is that activity of the church—in essence it is nothing else than an activity of Christ, exercised through the church—through which the church in this interim period, in which the end is postponed, calls the peoples of the earth to repentance and to faith in Christ, so that they may be made His disciples and through baptism be incorporated into the fellowship of those who await the coming of the kingdom' (p. 62). Except for a note of dispensationalism, clearly discernible in the expression, 'this interim period, in which the end is postponed', and perhaps less clearly in the clause, 'who await the coming of the kingdom', that definition certainly is acceptable. It is evident that evangelism embraces missions.

The term *evangelist* is properly used in various senses. The following pages contain a study of that term as it is employed in the New Testament. It will be shown that in the strict New Testament sense there are no evangelists at present. However, this is not a compelling reason for withholding that appellation from those who today make evangelism their lifework. In fact, it may be said without hesitation that every believer, being a prophet, as well as a priest and a king, by virtue of the universal office of all Christians, is correctly described as an evangelist.

Sad to say, much of present-day evangelism is man-centred. Far too often the limelight is turned full upon the evangelist – his personality, his eloquence, his ability as an organizer, the story of his conversion, the hardships which he has endured, the number of his converts, in some instances the miracles of healing allegedly performed by him. At other times attention is focused on those who are being evangelised – their large numbers, their sorry plight as exemplified by poverty, disease and immorality, their supposed yearning for the gospel of salvation, and, worst of all, the good that is said to dwell in them and to enable them to exercise saving faith of their own free, although unregenerate, volition. And how often the welfare of man, whether temporal or eternal, is made the sole end of evangelism!

The following study is a plea for *God-centred*, in contradistinction to man-centred, evangelism. In other words, it presents a *theology* of evangelism. And this theology is based squarely, as every theology must be, on the infallible

Word of God. Holy Scripture demands an evangelism which is of God, through God, and unto God (Rom. 11:36). Precisely that is the thrust of this volume.

The reader will soon discover that the theology here advocated is the Reformed theology. So it is, and so it must be. It is my firm conviction that the only theology contained in the Bible is the Reformed theology. However, I wish it understood that by the *Reformed theology* I mean not merely that which distinguishes it from more or less variant interpretations of Christianity, but also that which it has in common with these. For example, the Reformed theology includes the doctrine of the Trinity, that of the deity of Christ, and that of the substitutionary atonement as well as the so-called five points of Calvinism: absolute predestination, total depravity, particular atonement, irresistible grace, and the eternal security of believers. For me the Reformed faith is at once the purest and the most comprehensive of Christian theologies. It has the distinction of being based on the whole of Scripture. Its glory is that it embraces 'all the counsel of God' (Acts 20:27).

It was my privilege for some years to teach courses for ministerial students in 'Principles of Christian Missions' and 'Environmental Evangelism'. This book is not a reproduction of either of those courses, but rather a presentation of the heart of both.

Except where otherwise indicated, the Scripture quotations in this volume are from the Authorized King James Version. I am grateful to the Division of Christian Education of the National Council of the Churches of Christ in the United States of America for permission to quote occasionally from the Revised Standard Version. I am indebted to the New York *World-Telegram* and the *Sun* for certain statistics taken from the 1961 *World Almanac* and to the Presbyterian and Reformed Publishing Company of Philadelphia for permission to quote the aforesaid definition of *missions*.

R. B. KUIPER

Contents

1: God the Author of Evangelism

The Triune God as Author of Evangelism

Evangelism has its roots in eternity.

Theologians speak of the *pactum salutis*, made from everlasting by the three persons of the Godhead. The term *pactum salutis* may be translated either *covenant of redemption* or *council of redemption*. The writer prefers the latter rendering because the term *covenant* is used generally in theology to designate an agreement made by God with man and historically administered. Be that as it may, the truth of the matter is that the Father, the Son, and the Holy Spirit before the world was, unitedly planned the salvation of sinners.

In that plan God the Father was to send His Son into the world to redeem it, God the Son was voluntarily to come into the world in order to merit salvation by His obedience unto death, God the Holy Spirit was to apply salvation to sinners by the instilling of renewing grace within them.

Scripture plainly teaches the reality of this council of redemption. Especially in the writings of John, the Father is repeatedly said to have sent the Son. For but one example, 'Herein is love, not that we loved God, but that he loved us, and sent his Son to be the propitiation for our sins' (I John 4:10). Christ spoke of a commission given Him by the Father. For instance, toward the close of His earthly ministry He reported, as it were, to the Father: 'I have glorified thee on the earth; I have finished the work which thou gavest me to do' (John 17:4). In such a passage, among others, as Isaiah 53:12 prominent mention is made of the reward given by the Father to the Son for His accomplished work: 'Therefore will I divide him a portion with the great, and he shall divide the spoil with the strong; because he hath poured out his soul unto death; and he was numbered with the transgressors; and he bare the sin of many, and made intercession for the transgressors.' Just as clearly does Scripture teach that the Holy Spirit was sent by the Father and the Son. Jesus promised His disciples 'the Holy Ghost, whom', he said, 'the Father will send in my name' (John 14:26), and He described the third person of the Trinity as 'the Comforter, whom I will send you from the Father' (John 15:26).

In short, before the world was, the Triune God formed a plan of salvation to be executed in its several reciprocally distributed parts by the Father as Sender and Principal, by the Son as Sent, Mediator, and Sender, and by the Holy Spirit as Sent and Applier.

It follows that the Triune God is the author of salvation. And, inasmuch as He has executed in time the eternal plan of salvation, has revealed its execution in the gospel, and has ordained the gospel as the indispensable means of salvation, it is no less clear that the Triune God is the author of evangelism.

The Father as Author of Evangelism

God the Father is the author of evangelism.

He conceived evangelism in eternity.

Likewise in eternity He commissioned the Son to merit salvation for sinners by His substitutionary death on the accursed cross and by His rendering to the Father on behalf of sinners that perfect obedience the reward of which is eternal life.

He inspired prophets of old to foretell the coming of the Son of God in the flesh and to predict that through suffering He would enter into His glory (Luke 24:26). Through the evangelical prophet Isaiah He depicted the suffering 'servant of Jehovah' (Isa. 53), issued the universal gospel invitation, 'Look unto me, and be ye saved, all the ends of the earth: for I am God, and there is none else' (Isa. 45:22), and foretold the glorious day when 'the earth shall be full of the knowledge of the Lord, as the waters cover the sea' (Isa. 11:9).

He ordained the bloody sacrifices of the old dispensation to foreshadow the Son's saving sacrifice on Calvary's cross.

'When the fulness of the time was come' he 'sent forth his Son, made of a woman, made under the law, to redeem them that were under the law', in order that His people 'might receive the adoption of sons' (Gal. 4:4, 5).

At the beginning of the God-man's public ministry the Father sent down upon Him the Holy Spirit in the form of a dove (Luke 3:22) and thus qualified Him for his mediatorial labours. He anointed Him 'to preach the gospel to the poor, to heal the brokenhearted, to preach deliverance to the captives and recovery of sight to the blind, to set at liberty them that are bruised, to preach the acceptable year of the Lord' (Luke 4:18, 19).

He gave, He surrendered, He sacrificed, His only begotten Son in order that whosoever believes on Him should not perish but have life everlasting (John 3:16).

He sustained His Son in bearing the inestimable burden of the wrath of the holy and just God against the sin of all mankind so that, when the Son was forsaken of God and in that forsakenness suffered the anguish of very hell, He still clung to the Father as 'my God' (Matt. 27:46).

By raising the Son from the dead the Father put the stamp of His unqualified approval on the finished work of the Son, for He was raised, not merely that we might be justified, but because we had been justified by His vicarious death (Rom. 4:25).

Because the Son 'became obedient unto death, even the death of the cross', the Father 'hath highly exalted him, and given him a name which is above every name: that at the name of Jesus every knee should bow, of things in heaven, and things in earth, and things under the earth; and that every tongue should confess that Jesus Christ is Lord, to the glory of God the Father' (Phil. 2:8-11).

At Pentecost God the Father imparted to the church the power of the Holy Spirit in order that it might witness of the things of Christ 'in Jerusalem, and in all Judea, and in Samaria, and unto the uttermost part of the earth' (Acts 1:8).

The Son as Author of Evangelism

God the Son is the author of evangelism.

Although 'being in the form of God', He 'thought it not robbery to be equal with God', yet, voluntarily 'he made himself of no reputation, and took upon him the form of a servant, and was made in the likeness of men' (Phil. 2:6, 7), in order that He might accomplish the saving work which the Father had commissioned Him to do. At His coming into the world He said: 'Lo, I come (in the volume of the book it is written of me) to do thy will, O God' (Heb. 10:7).

He 'became obedient unto death, even the death of the cross' (Phil. 2:8). Thus dying the death of an accursed

[16]

one, He redeemed from the curse of God such as had not continued in all things which are written in the book of the law (Gal. 3 : 10, 13). By so doing He brought into being the very heart of the gospel. As 'the Lamb of God that taketh away the sin of the world' (John 1 : 29) He created the evangel.

He proclaimed the gospel through prophets of old in anticipation of His atoning death. They were but His mouthpieces. It was He who went and preached to Noah's disobedient contemporaries when the longsuffering of God waited while the ark was being prepared (I Peter 3 : 18–20). When holy men of old 'prophesied of the grace that should come', it was 'the Spirit of Christ' within them which 'testified beforehand the sufferings of Christ, and the glory that should follow' (I Peter 1 : 10, 11).

In the days of His flesh He proclaimed the gospel of the kingdom of God (Matt. 13), of the love of the heavenly Father for His wayward child (Luke 15 : 11–24), of 'the Son of man', the king, by appointment of the Ancient of days, of a universal and everlasting kingdom (Dan. 7 : 13, 14), who condescended 'to seek and to save that which was lost' (Luke 19 : 10), even publicans and sinners, the dregs of society. And, although He bade the twelve, whom He sent forth to preach the gospel, to restrict their evangelistic activity to 'the lost sheep of the house of Israel' (Matt. 10 : 6), He Himself brought the gospel to Samaritans (John 4).

Having died and risen again and thus ushered in a new dispensation, He charged His apostles and the church of all ages: 'All power is given unto me in heaven and on earth. Go ye therefore, and teach all nations, baptizing them in the name of the Father, and of the Son, and of the Holy Ghost; teaching them to observe all things whatsoever I have commanded you.' And for their encouragement in the performance of so colossal a task He added: 'Lo, I am with you alway, even unto the end of the world' (Matt. 28:18–20).

It was the Son of God who, at the gate of Damascus, stopped Saul of Tarsus, turned him from a persecutor of the church into the greatest Christian missionary of all time, and said concerning him: 'He is a chosen vessel unto me to bear my name before the Gentiles, and kings, and the children of Israel' (Acts 9:15).

At Pentecost the Holy Spirit was poured out. He worked mightily both in those who spoke and in those that heard. The disciples now received power to be Christ's witnesses throughout the world (Acts 1:8). And of those who heard, some three thousand were converted and baptized. It was the Son of God who had merited the Spirit for the church and now poured Him out upon the church. Said Peter in his Pentecostal sermon: 'Being by the right hand of God exalted, and having received of the Father the promise of the Holy Ghost, he hath shed forth this which ye now see and hear' (Acts 2:33).

Every preacher of the gospel today speaks in Christ's name; rather, Christ preaches through him as his ambassador. All evangelists can say with Paul: 'We pray you in Christ's stead, be ye reconciled to God' (II Cor. 5:20).

Truly, 'the Son of God, out of the whole human race, from the beginning to the end of the world, gathers, defends, and preserves for Himself, by His Spirit and Word, in the unity of the faith, a church chosen to everlasting life' (*The Heidelberg Catechism*, Lord's Day XXI, Answer 54).

In conclusion let it be stressed that the Son of God not merely stands at the head of that class of men who are known as missionaries or evangelists, but that as missionary or evangelist He is in a class entirely by himself. He is incomparable. He created the gospel. He Himself is the central theme of the gospel. In the final analysis He is the one and only preacher of the gospel. He applies the gospel efficaciously by the Holy Spirit. And He Himself has no need of the gospel. All that can be said of the Son of God alone.

The Holy Spirit as Author of Evangelism

God the Holy Spirit is the author of evangelism.

When holy men of old foretold the birth, the ministry, the death, and the resurrection of the Saviour and committed their prophecies to writing, so that the Old Testament as well as the New is gospel, they were 'moved by the Holy Ghost' (II Peter 1:21).

At Pentecost the Holy Spirit empowered a little band of insignificant, ignorant, and feeble, but believing, men and women to undertake the stupendous task of conquering the world for Christ, their Lord. The power of the Spirit was appropriately symbolized by two of the greatest forces of nature – wind and fire. That power, let it be remembered, has never departed from the church and never will depart, for the Spirit was given, said Christ, 'that he may abide with you forever' (John 14:16). A second Pentecost is unthinkable. The outpouring of the Holy Spirit at Pentecost is as unique and once-for-all an event as was the incarnation of the Son of God.

Through the power of the Holy Spirit the church became a witnessing church. Not only was cowardly Peter converted into a courageous preacher, every disciple became an evangelist. 'They were all filled with the Holy

[19]

Ghost, and began to speak with other tongues, as the Spirit gave them utterance' (Acts 2:4).

There were present men 'out of every nation under heaven' (Acts 2:5), both 'Jews and proselytes' (Acts 2:10). Through the operation of the Holy Spirit in their hearts some three thousand of them were converted. These were received by baptism into the Christian church, as the first-fruits of the bountiful harvest that was to be gathered into the church in centuries to come out of 'every kindred and tongue and people and nation' (Rev. 5:9).

The Holy Spirit calls evangelists to their work and guides them in its performance. In the apostolic age He called and guided them by special revelations. To the church at Antioch in Syria, 'The Holy Ghost said, Separate me Barnabas and Saul for the work whereunto I have called them' (Acts 13:2). And Luke relates that Paul and his helpers 'were forbidden of the Holy Ghost to preach the word in Asia' and that 'the Spirit suffered them not' to go into Bithynia, but by a supernatural vision directed them to Macedonia (Acts 16:6–9). Now that special revelation is complete in the Scriptures of the Old and New Testaments, the manner of the Spirit's calling and leading is different; yet they are not a whit less real. He calls and leads by divine providence and by His gracious influence on the minds and hearts of those whom He would have sow the seed of the gospel and bring in the harvest. Jesus commanded the seventy, whom He sent into every city and place which He planned to visit: 'Pray ye the Lord of the harvest, that he would send forth labourers into his harvest' (Luke 10:1, 2). 'Now the Lord is that Spirit' (II Cor. 3:17).

The Holy Spirit opens doors for the spread of the gospel. By a marvellous providence He guided Paul to

Rome, the capital of the pagan world, where, though a prisoner, he preached the kingdom of God and taught those things which concern the Lord Jesus Christ 'with all confidence, no man forbidding him' (Acts 28:31). In consequence members even of Caesar's household were brought to faith in Christ(Phil 4:22). Those who proclaim the gospel may be bound, and often are, 'but the Word of God is not bound' (II Tim. 2:9) because the Spirit of God cannot be bound. And 'the king's heart is in the hand of the Lord as the rivers of water: he turneth it whithersoever he will' (Prov. 21:1). By His Spirit God often bends the wills of His bitterest foes to do His bidding so that the wrath of man is made to praise him (Ps. 76:10).

As the Spirit of truth, the third person of the Holy Trinity preserves the gospel. But for this activity of His, the gospel would long ago have been lost. The church itself would have destroyed it. The history of the church is replete with corruptions and rejections of the evangel. But the Spirit, who was poured out upon it at Pentecost, was to abide with it and in it for ever (John 14:16). For that reason, and only for that reason, has the church continued, and will it continue, as 'the pillar and ground of the truth' (I Tim. 3:15). To the end of time there will be a body of true believers proclaiming the true evangel.

Of the many who received the gospel as proclaimed by Peter at Jerusalem on the day of Pentecost not one was converted by the apostle's eloquence. Nor was anyone converted by the exercise of his own unregenerate will. Everyone that received the Word did so because of the operation within him of the irresistible grace of the Holy Spirit. Likewise at Philippi Lydia gave heed to the things spoken by Paul only because the Lord opened her heart (Acts 16:14). He did it by the working of His Spirit. In all

2: God's Infinite Love and Evangelism

'FOR GOD SO LOVED THE WORLD, THAT HE GAVE his only begotten Son, that whosoever believeth in him should not perish but have everlasting life' (John 3:16). That verse of Scripture has often, and for good reason, been denominated 'the heart of the evangel'.

Sovereign Love

The term *world* as used in John 3:16 presents a serious difficulty of exegesis. To name three proposed interpretations: some think it designates the elect, those whom God chose from the foundation of the world unto life eternal; others say it embraces all men individually, those who have lived on earth in the past, those who dwell there today, and those who remain to be born; still others insist that it refers to the sum total of creation, the plants and the animals, the rivers and the oceans, the mountains and the valleys, the planets and the stars, spirits and the powers of nature, as well as men.

Each of these interpretations lies open to serious objection. It is doubtful whether anywhere in Scripture *the world* is identified with the elect. While God, no doubt, loves all men, He does not bestow saving love on all alike; yet that truth is usually overlooked by proponents of the second of the aforenamed interpretations. And to say that God loves all things is to ignore the very nature of love, which is such that it can be bestowed only upon objects capable of requiting it.

[23]

A grave objection applies alike to all three of the aforesaid constructions of the term *world* in John 3:16. They are all of them attempts to measure the infinite love of God in finite terms. The elect constitute a great multitude which no man can number (Rev. 7:9); yet, their number is finite. Obviously, the entire population of the whole earth throughout all of history is finite. Even the universe, immense though it is beyond human imagination, is still finite. Only the Creator is infinite. And He is infinite in all His attributes, also in that of love. Just that is the point of John 3:16, for it not only tells us that the love of God is great but, as is indicated by the adverb 'so', it answers the question *how great* that love is. It is infinite. But to measure the infinite in terms of the finite is utterly impossible.

To illustrate, let us subtract a billion years from eternity. What is the remainder? Of course, it is eternity. And that can only mean that a billion years, no matter how long a time, in comparison with eternity are nothing.

To illustrate again, the physical prowess of the old-fashioned blacksmith was proverbial. Especially the muscles of his arms were wonderfully well developed. Someone, let us say, wishing to describe his great strength, says: 'This man is so strong that he can support a mustard seed in his extended palm.' What has he said? Obviously, he has made an exceedingly foolish statement. Yet it cannot be denied that he has said something, for some strength is required to uphold even a mustard seed. But when one states that the infinite love of God is so great that it embraces the whole of the finite universe, one has said precisely nothing.

In a sermon on John 3:16, included in the volume *The Saviour of the World*, that eminent theologian Benjamin

B. Warfield has insisted that 'the world' in John 3:16 must be qualitatively rather than quantitatively. The writer is convinced that Warfield was quite right. The emphasis falls, not on the size of the world, but on the sinful quality of the human race. It may be observed incidentally that this usage of the term is very frequent in the writings of John. The point, then, is not that the world is so big that it takes a great deal of love to embrace it but that the world is so bad that it takes an exceedingly great kind of love to love it at all.

John 3:16 makes an unimaginable declaration. It reveals the greatest marvel of history, an unfathomable mystery. It is that the holy God, in whose presence the very seraphs cover their faces with their wings because they cannot behold His resplendent holiness and, while doing so, cry out to one another: 'Holy, holy, holy, is the Lord of hosts: the whole earth is full of his glory' (Isa. 6:2, 3), loves sinful men, afflicted with spiritual leprosy, covered with leprosy from the crowns of their heads to the soles of their feet.

A most significant conclusion must now be drawn. The love of God which lies at the very heart of the evangel is *sovereign*. And that means that the divine love, unlike human love, is not dependent on its object. One human being, let us say, loves another. He does so because he sees something lovely in the other. And if the time should ever come that he would see nothing lovable in the other, he could not possibly continue to love him. Not so is the love of God. God loves such as are altogether despicable and wholly repulsive. The reason why God loves them lies not in them, but in God himself. And if the question be asked what it is in God that accounts for His love for sinners, all we can say is: 'God is love' (I John 4:8, 16). God loves sinners because He is who He is. God loves sinful men *sovereignly*.

Sacrificial Love

So great is God's sovereign love for sinners that He gave His only begotten Son.

Who can measure the love of God for His Son? It far surpasses the love of the best human father for his son. It is natural for a human father to love his son for the reason that his son is bone of his bone, flesh of his flesh, blood of his blood. He loves his son because he loves himself. Much is being said and written nowadays about 'selfless love'. It is ascribed to God and God's children. But the truth of the matter is that selfless love is non-existent. God loves Himself. For His own name's sake He does all that He does. Hence the Psalmist prayed: 'Help us, O God of our salvation, for the glory of thy name: and deliver us and purge away our sins, for thy name's sake' (Ps. 79:9), and The Highest Himself declared: 'I am the Lord; that is my name: and my glory will I not give to another' (Isa. 42: 8). Man, created as he was in God's image, also loves himself, and God put His stamp of approval on man's self-love, in contradistinction to selfishness, when He commanded him to love his neighbour as himself (Matt. 19:19). God the Father, then, loves the Son because He loves Himself. A human father, too, loves his son because he loves himself. But now observe the difference! While a human father shares the honour of parenthood with the mother and generations of grandparents, God shares that honour with no one. All the honour of parenthood is His. He is the eternal Father of the eternal Son. It follows that He loves His Son incomparably more than any human father can possibly love his son.

And who can describe the love of God for His *only begotten* Son? A human father loves an *only* son especially. But what a difference between the love of God for His only Son and the love of the best human father for his only son! Here, too, comparison is impossible. A father among men who in fact has but one son might, humanly speaking, have more sons than that one. But it is inconceivable that God the Father would have more sons than one, for all the fullness of divinity is expressed in the one Son of God. He could say: 'I and my Father are one' (John 10:30) and 'He that hath seen me hath seen the Father' (John 14:9). God, then, must love His only begotten Son with all the love of which the infinite heart of God alone is capable.

God so loved sinful men that for them He gave that Son of His love. Let no one think this merely means that the Son was a present of God to sinful humanity. Much more is implied in the word 'gave'. It means *surrendered, sacrificed*. And to what did God sacrifice His Son? To a life of deepest humiliation and to the bitter, shameful, and accursed death of the cross; that is to say, to nothing less than the anguish of hell. The crucified Christ was smitten with the curse of God, for it is written: 'Cursed is every one that hangeth on a tree' (Gal. 3:13). Therefore God forsook Him. That was hell itself. When He cried with a loud voice: 'My God, my God, why hast thou forsaken me?' (Matt. 27:46) He was at the very bottom of the bottomless pit.

John 3:16 makes the amazing, incomprehensible, unfathomably profound, well-nigh unbelievable, declaration that the holy God sovereignly loves hell-deserving sinners, and that He loves them so much that He was willing that His only begotten Son, whom He loves with

[27]

all the love of His infinite heart, should go to hell in their stead.

Saving Love

The love of God does not save all men. John 3:16 teaches unmistakably that only those who believe on the Son will have eternal life. The same truth looms exceedingly large throughout the New Testament.

It might be inferred that the love of God is less than infinite. But that inference would be wholly unwarranted, for it is based on the false assumption, previously refuted, that the infinite can be measured by the finite. If all human beings were to be saved, the number of the saved would still be finite. And the finite and the infinite are simply incomparable. In reality, the fact that believers, and only they, are saved is a further revelation of the infinitude of the divine love.

Being almighty, God could save all men by force. Being love, He has chosen to save by love instead. He wonderfully displays His love in the crucified Son. In the gospel He lovingly pleads with sinners to respond to that love by receiving the Son in faith. Because God saves by love, not by force, only believers are saved.

God might conceivably have sold salvation at a price commensurate with its worth, or have made it the reward for a perfect life. No man could have paid that price nor have led that life. In His love God sent the Son into the world to pay the whole price and to accomplish all the required work. On the basis of those merits God now offers salvation to men as a free gift which they may have for the taking. What inestimable love!

It has been said that because of the greatness of God's

love no man can perish everlastingly. That is a contradiction of the plain teaching of Scripture. It has also been said that the salvation of believers is a revelation of God's love, the damnation of unbelievers a manifestation of God's justice. That is true enough, but it is not the whole truth. The unbeliever spurns the love of God. If this love were small, it would be a small sin to ignore it. If this love is great, it is a great sin to reject it. But the fact is that this love is infinite. That makes the spurning of it a sin of infinite proportions. Precisely because the love of God is as great as it is, the unbeliever must suffer eternal punishment.

'Whosoever' believes on the Son of God will be saved – he whose sins are as scarlet or crimson (Isa. 1:18) as well as he whose sins are relatively less flagrant; the murderer, the kidnapper, and the prostitute as well as the respectable citizen. None of these can be saved without faith in the Christ. All alike will be saved if they believe on Him. Boundless love!

All who believe on the Son of God will receive 'eternal life'. Instead of consigning them to their just desert, eternal banishment from the presence of God, the God of infinite love will bestow upon them the fullest bliss of heaven, communion with God, which is man's highest good, throughout the never-ending ages of eternity.

And, not to be forgotten, although it is customary in orthodox circles to speak of 'saving faith', strictly speaking, it is not faith that saves. God does the saving through the instrumentality of faith, imparted in loving sovereignty by the Holy Spirit. For 'no man can say that Jesus is the Lord, but by the Holy Ghost' (I Cor. 12:3). The faith by which the sinner appropriates Christ and all His saving benefits is itself a gift of divine love (Eph. 2:8). And, while

Scripture insists that salvation is *by* or *through* faith, it never says that salvation is *on account of* faith. Faith is, as it were, the hand by which the sinner receives the salvation proffered by God. As a beggar, when accepting whatever is given him, does not thereby merit the gift, so faith in no way merits salvation. It is and remains a free gift of the God of infinite love.

Universal Love

Although the emphasis of John 3 : 16 is on the sinfulness of the world, not on its size, and consequently on the sovereignty of God's love rather than its comprehensiveness, it may not be inferred that the love of God is less than universal. Nor may that inference be drawn from the fact that the saving love of God is not bestowed on each and every individual. God's love is indeed universal, and its universal character is exhibited unmistakably in Scripture.

When certain Samaritans had come to believe in Jesus, they exclaimed: 'This is indeed the Christ, the Saviour of the world' (John 4 : 42). And when certain Greeks wanted to see Jesus, He was deeply moved and said: 'I, if I be lifted up from the earth, will draw all men unto me' (John 12 : 32). In these passages, as in a great many others, Christ is described as the Saviour, not of Jews only, but of men from every tribe and nation; in short, of humanity. That is one phase of the universalism of the new dispensation. It presupposes God's universal love.

In I John 2 : 2 we are told that Christ is 'the propitiation for our sins; and not for ours only, but also for the whole world' (ASV). This can only mean that the whole world of man, the human race, will be saved collectively, although not distributively. That is to say, not every individual will be saved, but those who are saved will constitute the true humanity. Renewed humanity will be real humanity. Nor may the obvious fact be overlooked that the world of *sinful* humanity on which, according to John 3:16, God bestows His saving love is the world of *humanity*. That is another aspect of universalism. And again it presupposes God's universal love.

The universalism of Scripture is not thus exhausted. It extends farther. The God of love has ordained that the gospel shall be preached everywhere, and He informs us in His Word that He desires the salvation of every sinner reached by the gospel. He gives that assurance in both the Old and the New Testament. Swearing by Himself, God declares by Ezekiel: 'As I live, saith the Lord God, I have no pleasure in the death of the wicked; but that the wicked turn from his way and live' (Ezek. 33:11). Paul the apostle asserts that God 'will have all men to be saved, and to come unto the knowledge of the truth' (I Tim. 2:4). The apostle Peter affirms that the Lord 'is long-suffering to us-ward, not willing that any should perish, but that all should come to repentance' (II Peter 3:9). The same note of universal love sounds forth loud and clear in the Saviour's invitation: 'Come unto me, all ye that labour and are heavy laden, and I will give you rest' (Matt. 11:28).

It is evident that sinners everywhere are to be told that God will be pleased to save them if they repent and believe. Yet that is not all. They are to be told that the God of infinite love will be pleased to see them repent, believe, and be saved.

3: God's Sovereign Election and Evangelism

FROM EVERLASTING GOD HAS FOREORDAINED all that comes to pass, the eternal destiny of men included. The divine decree concerning that destiny the Bible calls *predestination*. That aspect of predestination which is most prominent in Scripture is known as *election*. It is taught in such a passage, among many others, as Ephesians 1:4-6, 11: 'According as he hath chosen us in him before the foundation of the world, that we should be holy and without blame before him in love: having predestinated us unto the adoption of children by Jesus Christ to himself, according to the good pleasure of his will, to the praise of the glory of his grace, wherein he hath made us accepted in the beloved . . . in whom also we have obtained an inheritance, being predestinated according to the purpose of him who worketh all things after the counsel of his own will.'

No council of churches has deliberated on this subject at such length and with such painstaking regard for the Word of God as did the Synod of Dort, at which the Reformed churches of practically all of Europe were represented, in the years 1618 and 1619. That body of divines came to the following conclusion: 'Election is the unchangeable purpose of God whereby, before the foundation of the world, He has out of mere grace, according to the sovereign good pleasure of His own will, chosen from the whole human race, which had fallen through their own fault from their primitive state of rectitude into sin and destruction, a certain number of persons to redemption in

Christ, whom He from eternity appointed the Mediator and Head of the elect and the foundation of salvation' (*The Canons of Dort*, I, 7). Chapter III of *The Westminster Confession of Faith*, the most mature, no doubt, of all Reformed creeds, and rated by many as the greatest creed of Christendom, is no less explicit on this theme.

As we seek to relate to evangelism this phase of what is usually termed 'the secret will of God', it behoves us to remember that we are dealing with a profound mystery, that we are here on holy ground where angels fear to tread, that finite man cannot begin to comprehend the infinite God, and that therefore we must be sober, scrupulously avoiding human speculation and abiding strictly by the sure Word of God.

The Loving Sovereignty of Election

The ground of election did not lie in those who were chosen, but in God Himself. It is not true, as is sometimes said, that God chose certain persons unto salvation because He foreknew that they would believe in Christ. He did indeed foreknow that, as He foreknew all that was to occur in time, but that foreknowledge was not the reason for His choice. Saving faith is a gift of the electing God to His elect by which their election is realized (Eph. 2:8). Instead of being the ground of election, it is one of its consequences. The Bible states explicitly that God chose 'according to the good pleasure of his will' (Eph. 1:5). That can only mean that He chose sovereignly.

The sovereign character of election appears also in the fact that it was unconditional. God did not choose certain persons to eternal life because He foreknew that they would believe in Christ, but neither did He decree that certain sinners would be saved *if* they should believe in Christ. God decreed that certain men would be saved through faith in Christ. Therefore Paul informed the believers at Thessalonica: 'God hath from the beginning chosen you to salvation through sanctification of the Spirit and belief of the truth' (II Thess. 2.13). Faith, then, is a fruit of election, not a condition. 'Although God knows whatsoever may or can come to pass upon all supposed conditions, yet hath He not decreed anything because He foresaw it as future, or as that which would come to pass upon such conditions' (*The Westminster Confession of Faith*, III, 2).

Again, the sovereignty of election is manifest in its unchangeableness. God has solemnly declared: 'My counsel shall stand, and I will do all my pleasure' (Isa. 46:10). Paul asserted: 'Whom he did predestinate, them he also called; and whom he called, them he also justified; and whom he justified, them he also glorified' (Rom. 8:30). Every one of God's elect is sure to attain to heavenly glory. The Westminster divines were right when they affirmed that the elect 'are particularly and unchangeably designed; and their number is so certain and definite, that it cannot be either increased or diminished' (*The Westminster Confession of Faith*, III, 4). So was the Synod of Dort right in ascribing election to God's 'unchangeable good pleasure' (*The Canons of Dort*, I, 11). God, 'with whom can be no variableness, neither shadow that is cast by turning' (James 1:17 ASV), will not alter His own decree. Feeble man cannot alter it. Neither can Satan.

Let no one think that God chose certain persons arbitrarily unto salvation. Nothing that God does is done arbitrarily. He does all that He does, because He is who He is. What, then, was it in God that moved Him, so to speak, to choose certain persons unto life everlasting? That question God has answered unequivocally in His Word. He chose them because He loved them. Romans 8:29 says: 'Whom he did foreknow, he also did predestinate to be conformed to the image of his Son', and I Peter 1:2 speaks of such as are 'elect according to the foreknowledge of God'. In both these places *knowledge* clearly has that pregnant meaning which it so often has in Scripture; namely, *love. Foreknowledge*, then, is *love from eternity*. God loved His elect from everlasting. For that reason He elected them to eternal life. And if the question be asked why God from eternity loved unto salvation some men in distinction from others, it behoves us humbly to confess ignorance. Only to a most limited extent can we think God's thoughts after Him. His thoughts are not our thoughts. As the heavens are higher than the earth, so are God's thoughts higher than our thoughts (Isa. 55:8, 9). Yet, this we know: not one was deserving of God's love. All, having sinned in Adam, were deserving of death, even eternal death. All were 'by nature the children of wrath' (Eph. 2:3). If God had permitted all men to perish everlastingly, all would have received their just deserts and not one would have had cause for complaint. For that reason it is unspeakably presumptuous for any man to complain that in his counsel of predestination God chose only some and passed others by. Here the scathing words of the apostle apply: 'Nay but, O man, who art thou that repliest against God? Shall the thing formed say to him that formed it, Why hast thou made me thus? Hath not the potter power over the clay, of the same lump to make one vessel unto honour, and another unto dishonour?' (Rom. 9:20, 21). Rather than find fault with God for His altogether righteous dealings with certain hell-deserving sinners, let us adore Him for this eternal, gracious, saving love for others just as deserving of damnation.

Believers are told that God chose them *in Christ* (Eph. 1:4). On the precise meaning of that phrase there has been much debate among theologians. By now a few conclusions may safely be drawn. Obviously, the thought is excluded that God chose without reference to Christ certain sinners unto salvation and, having done that, proceeded to plan the realization of their salvation through Christ. That would make Christ a mere means in the execution of the decree of election. We are not told that the elect were chosen unto salvation through Christ, but that they were chosen in Christ unto salvation. It is just as clear that the phrase *in Christ* cannot mean that, as Mediator between God and sinners, Christ, so to speak, induced the Father to choose certain sinners unto everlasting life. That interpretation would contradict John 3:16, which states that God was moved by love for sinners to send His Son into the world for the performance of His mediatorial work. That God chose His own in Christ must mean – whatever more may be implied – that in the counsel of election God beheld them as being in Christ, His beloved Son; in short, that He chose them in the love wherewith He loves the Son. In other words, the statement of Ephesians 1:5, 'He destined us in love' (RSV) is parallel to, and explanatory of, the statement of the immediately preceding verse, that God chose us in Christ.

Evangelism Required by Election

Occasionally it is suggested that election makes evangelism superfluous. The question is asked: 'If the decree of election is unchangeable and therefore renders the

[36]

salvation of the elect completely certain, what need have they of the gospel? Will not the elect be saved whether or not they hear the evangel?'

The premise of that argumentation is altogether true. Divine election makes the salvation of the elect unalterably certain. But the conclusion drawn from that premise reveals a serious misunderstanding of the divine sovereignty as expressed in the decree of election.

While election is from everlasting, the truth may not be lost out of sight that its realization is a process in time. In that process numerous factors play a part. One of those factors is the evangel. And it is a most significant factor.

The sovereignty of God is not to be equated with His almighty power. God is indeed almighty. Significantly, the brief *Apostles' Creed* ascribes that attribute to Him, not once, but twice. If He wished, God might by sheer force lift up His elect to heaven and likewise by sheer force thrust the non-elect down to hell. But He does nothing of the kind. Foreordination is not compulsion, nor does certainty preclude freedom. No one was ever converted to Christianity by force. Every true convert turns willingly, his willingness, to be sure, being a gift of God, bestowed in the new birth. God deals with men as rational and moral creatures, as free agents. Therefore He reasons and pleads with the unsaved through the gospel. He would 'persuade' men (II Cor. 5:11). And in the case of the elect He applies the gospel to their hearts in a saving way through the Holy Spirit.

Let no one suppose that God's sovereign decree concerns only ends, to the exclusion of means. It cannot be said too emphatically that God has foreordained *all* that comes to pass. *All* embraces means as well as ends. To illustrate, God not merely foreordained that a certain farmer would reap five thousand bushels of wheat in the summer of 1961; He foreordained that that farmer would harvest that amount of wheat as the result of much hard work. Likewise, God did not merely decree that a certain sinner would inherit eternal life, but He decreed that that sinner would receive eternal life through faith in Christ and that he would obtain faith in Christ through the gospel.

The sovereignty of God may not be construed so as to rule out the responsibility of man. Because the ablest and most learned theologians and philosophers have proved unable to reconcile divine sovereignty and human responsibility with each other before the bar of human reason, the danger is ever imminent that one of these will be stressed at the expense, even to the exclusion, of the other. But the Bible teaches both with great emphasis, and he who in humble faith accepts the Bible as the infallible Word of God, will stress mightily one as well as the other. Therefore, the preacher of the gospel must tell the sinner, not merely that salvation is by sovereign grace alone, but also that, in order to be saved, he must believe in Jesus Christ as Saviour and Lord. On the one hand, he must proclaim that God's elect are sure to be saved; on the other hand, he must issue the warning that he who does not believe the Son will not see life, but the wrath of God will abide on him (John 3:36). Even the elect need that admonition, for it is part and parcel of God's way of bringing them to salvation.

A most significant conclusion is now warranted. Instead of rendering evangelism superfluous, *election demands evangelism*. All of God's elect must be saved. Not one of them may perish. And the gospel is the means by which God bestows saving faith upon them. In fact, it is the only means which God employs to that end. 'Faith cometh by hearing, and hearing by the Word of God' (Rom. 10:17).

Here let it be observed that, paradoxical though it may seem, election is universal. To be sure, election is the choice of certain persons out of a larger number to ever-lasting life. Thus election spells particularism. Yet, in a real sense election is universal. God has His elect in every nation and also in every age. The church consists of 'elect from every nation', and in no period of history have God's elect perished from the earth, nor will that occur in the future. God wants the evangel proclaimed throughout the world and throughout time in order that the sum total of His elect may be gathered in. Again let it be said, *election demands evangelism*.

The same truth may be viewed from still another angle. Scripture teaches that election was unto good works. Said Paul: 'We are his workmanship, created in Christ Jesus for good works, which God afore prepared that we should walk in them' (Eph. 2:10 ASV). And Scripture teaches specifically that election was unto witnessing. Said Peter: 'Ye are a chosen generation . . . that ye should show forth the praises of him who hath called you out of dark-ness into his marvellous light' (I Peter 2:9). God chose certain persons, not only that they might go to heaven when they die, but also that they might be His witnesses while here on earth. Once more let it be said, *election de-mands evangelism*.

An equally significant conclusion is that *election guarantees that evangelism will result in genuine conver-sions*. The preacher of the gospel has no way of telling who in his audience belongs to the elect and who does not. But God knows. And God is sure to bless His Word to the hearts of His elect unto salvation. Just when it will please

God to do that in the case of an elect individual, we do not know, but He most certainly will do it before that person's death. So certain as it is that all of God's elect will be saved, precisely so certain is it that the word of the gospel will not return to God void (cf. Isa. 55:11).

Preterition and the Gospel Offer

Election has its obverse side. If God chose out of the fallen human race a limited number to everlasting life, it is obvious that He passed others by, leaving them in their lost estate and decreeing their damnation because of their sins. Theologically that aspect of predestination is known as preterition, rejection, or reprobation. It has been argued that this doctrine rules out the universal and sincere offer of the gospel. If God decreed from eternity that some men would perish everlastingly, it is said to be inconceivable that He would in time sincerely invite all without distinction to everlasting life.

In an attempt to refute that argumentation the observation is sometimes made that the human preacher has no way of knowing who are God's elect and who are not, and that therefore he has no choice but to proclaim the gospel indiscriminately to all. True though that observation is, it is not at all to the point. The question is whether God, who knows infallibly who are His elect and who are not, makes a sincere offer of salvation to all to whom the gospel comes.

The all-important fact is that the Word of God teaches unmistakably both divine reprobation and the universality as well as the sincerity of the gospel offer. Reprobation is undeniably taught in Romans 9:21, 22: 'Hath not the potter power over the clay, of the same lump to make one vessel unto honour, and another unto dishonour? What if God, willing to show his wrath, and to make his power known, endured with much longsuffering the vessels of wrath fitted to destruction . . . ?' and in I Peter 2:8, where mention is made of 'them which stumble at the word, being disobedient, whereunto also they were appointed'. As was shown in the foregoing chapter, the universal and sincere offer of the gospel is assuredly taught in Ezekiel 33:11, II Peter 3:9, and elsewhere.

We may as well admit – in fact it must be admitted – that these teachings cannot be reconciled with each other by human reason. As far as human logic is concerned, they rule one another out. However, the acceptance of either to the exclusion of the other stands condemned as rationalism. Not human reason, but God's infallible Word, is the norm of truth. That Word contains many paradoxes. The classical example is that of divine sovereignty and human responsibility. The two teachings now under consideration also constitute a striking paradox. To destroy a Scriptural paradox by rejecting one of its elements is to place human logic above the divine Word. To subject human logic to the divine *logos* is the part of child-like faith.

It is noteworthy that in the history of the Christian church those theologians who have been most insistent on the truth of divine rejection have also upheld most emphatically the universal and sincere offer of the gospel. A few examples follow.

It is generally known that John Calvin taught divine reprobation. At times he even took a so-called supralapsarian position; that is to say, he held that the decree of predestination logically preceded the decrees of creation and the fall. Yet, in commenting on Ezekiel 18:23, which parallels Ezekiel 33:11, he said: 'God desires nothing more earnestly than that those who were perishing and rushing to destruction should return into the way of safety.' He proceeded: 'If any should object—then there is no election of God, by which He has predestinated a fixed number to salvation—the answer is at hand: the prophet does not here speak of God's secret counsel, but only recalls miserable men from despair, that they may apprehend the hope of pardon, and repent and embrace the offered salvation. If any one again objects—this is making God act with duplicity—the answer is ready, that God always wishes the same thing, though by different ways, and in a manner inscrutable to us. Although, therefore, God's will is simple, yet great variety is involved in it, as far as our senses are concerned. Besides, it is not surprising that our eyes should be blinded by intense light, so that we cannot certainly judge how God wishes all to be saved, and yet has devoted all the reprobate to eternal destruction, and wishes them to perish. While we look now through a glass darkly, we should be content with the measure of our intelligence.'

The Canons of Dort teach the decree of reprobation unmistakably. Say they: 'What peculiarly tends to illustrate and recommend to us the eternal and unmerited grace of election is the express testimony of Sacred Scripture that not all, but some only, are elected, while others are passed by in the eternal decree; whom God, out of His sovereign, most just, irreprehensible, and unchangeable good pleasure, has decided to leave in the common misery into which they have wilfully plunged themselves, and not to bestow upon them saving faith and the grace of conversion; but, permitting them in His just judgment to follow their own ways, at last, for the declaration of His justice, to condemn and punish them for ever, not only on account of their unbelief, but also for all their other sins' (I, 15). Yet the *Canons* also insist: 'As many as are called by the gospel are unfeignedly called. For God has most earnestly and truly declared in His Word what is acceptable to Him; namely, that those who are called should come unto Him' (III–IV, 8).

Upholding the aforesaid teaching of Dort on reprobation, Herman Bavinck denied both that faith was the cause of election and that sin was the cause of rejection, and insisted that both election and rejection were rooted in the sovereign good pleasure of God. To be very exact, he taught that God sovereignly decreed from eternity that some men would escape the punishment of their sins, others would not (*Gereformeerde Dogmatiek*, II, 399). But in the same standard work that well-balanced Calvinist also asserted: 'Although through calling salvation becomes the portion of but few . . . it [calling] nevertheless has great value and significance for those also who reject it. It is for all without exception proof of God's infinite love and seals the statement that He has no pleasure in the death of the sinner, but therein that he turn and live' (IV, 7).

The Presentation of Election to the Unsaved

The question can hardly be suppressed what place, if any, the doctrine of election should occupy in preaching to the unsaved.

Both Scripture and the Reformed confessions tell us that the truth of election is intended primarily for believers. The purpose which it serves for them is admirably summed up in *The Canons of Dort*. Say they: 'The sense and certainty of this election afford to the children of God additional matter for daily humiliation before Him, for adoring the depth of His mercies, for cleansing themselves and rendering grateful returns of ardent love to Him who first manifested so great love toward them' (I, 13).

An old illustration makes abundantly clear what use should *not* be made of the doctrine of election in dealing with the unsaved. We may speak of the house of salvation. The foundation of that house is the divine decree of election, the entrance is Christ. Said He: 'I am the door' (John 10:9). As those who by the grace of God are within the house invite those without to enter, shall they point them to the foundation or to the door? The answer is self-evident. And so, when the Philippian jailer asked Paul and Silas what he had to do to be saved, they did not advise him to seek to discover whether he might be numbered among the elect; they commanded him to believe on the Lord Jesus Christ (Acts 16:31).

Does it follow that men should be kept in ignorance of election until they have received Christ in faith? The answer to that question must, of course, be negative. To be sure, the Westminster Assembly was on good ground in warning that 'the doctrine of this high mystery of predestination is to be handled with special prudence and care' (*The Westminster Confession of Faith*, III, 8), but this cannot mean that it should be kept hidden from the unsaved. Contrariwise, they should be warned against distorting this truth and exhorted to its proper use.

Specifically, they should be told that election spells salvation by divine grace, that human merit is out of the question, and that therefore there is hope for the chief of sinners; that the God of election sincerely, cordially, urgently even, invites every sinner to salvation; that predestination, far from excluding human responsibility, definitely includes it so that all who hear the gospel proclaimed are in sacred duty bound to believe, and, God not being the cause of unbelief as He is the cause of faith, those who persist in unbelief perish wholly through their own fault; that the decree of election is not secret in the sense that none can be certain of belonging to the elect, but that, on the contrary, faith in Christ being the fruit and also the proof of election, one can be just as sure of being numbered among the elect as of being a believer; that the house into which they are invited has an eternal, unmovable foundation, so that he who enters, though all hell should assail him, cannot possibly perish but will most certainly inherit everlasting life.

4: God's Gracious Covenant and Evangelism

WHEN MAN DWELT IN THE GARDEN OF EDEN, God warned him on pain of death not to eat of the fruit of the tree of the knowledge of good and evil (Gen. 2:17). It was implied that, if he remained obedient, he would receive eternal life; that is to say, he would rise from the state of being able to sin and, having sinned, to die, to that of being unable either to sin or to die. That arrangement – if such it may be called – has been denominated *the covenant of works*. The name is not beyond reproach, for God's making this disposal was a matter of unmerited love and, hence of pure *grace*. Be that as it may, man fell and in consequence became so depraved that henceforth perfect obedience to God was for him an impossibility.

No sooner had that transpired than God promised to fallen man a Saviour who would pay the penalty which man had incurred by his disobedience and would render to God on behalf of man that perfect obedience which was from the beginning, and continued to be, the condition of life eternal. All that God required of the sinner in order to share in that salvation was faith in the Saviour; that is, living faith manifesting itself in works of love. This arrangement is commonly and correctly denominated *the covenant of grace*.

The covenant of grace was implicit in the so-called prot-evangelium of Genesis 3:15. Immediately after the fall of man God spoke to the serpent: 'I will put enmity between thee and the woman, and between thy seed and her seed; it shall bruise thy head, and thou shalt bruise his heel.' The same covenant was formally established by God with Abraham. Said God to His friend: 'I will establish my covenant between me and thee and thy seed after thee in their generations for an everlasting covenant, to be a God unto thee and to thy seed after thee' (Gen. 17:7). There were steps in the revelation of the covenant; in other words, it was revealed progressively. This becomes abundantly clear from the promise of Jeremiah 31:31–34, which in Hebrews 8:8–12 is appropriated for the post-Pentecostal church. That promise reads: 'Behold the days come, saith the Lord, that I will make a new covenant with the house of Israel, and with the house of Judah: not according to the covenant that I made with their fathers in the day that I took them by the hand to bring them out of the land of Egypt; which my covenant they brake, although I was an husband unto them, saith the Lord: but this shall be the covenant that I will make with the house of Israel: After those days, saith the Lord, I will put my law in their inward parts, and will write it in their hearts; and will be their God, and they shall be my people. And they shall teach no more every man his brother, saying, Know the Lord; for they shall all know me, from the least of them unto the greatest of them, saith the Lord; for I will forgive their iniquity and I will remember their sin no more.' Although revealed in stages, the one covenant of grace is continuous throughout the ages. It embraces believers of all times. 'They which are of faith, the same are the children of Abraham' (Gal. 3:7). Believers are told: 'If ye be Christ's, then are ye Abraham's seed, and heirs according to the promise' (Gal. 3:29).

The Covenant and Election

In a study of the bearing of the covenant of grace on evangelism it may prove helpful first to relate the covenant to the decree of election.

Christian theology consists largely of pairs or couplets of complementary truths. The doctrine of divine election and the doctrine of the covenant of grace constitute such a couplet. The two are to be distinguished from each other; but it goes without saying that they cannot nullify each other, for both are taught unmistakably in God's infallible Word, and truth is never self-contradictory. It is a matter of great importance that their complementary character be recognized.

Election took place in eternity. The covenant, although conceived in eternity, was established in time and is administered throughout history.

In election man was wholly passive. In the covenant man becomes active. He exercises active faith in Christ and, actuated by that faith, leads a life of grateful obedience.

Theologically expressed, while election was monopleuric, or one-sided, the covenant of grace is both monopleuric and dipleuric, or two-sided. God elected certain sinners to salvation. In no sense did they elect themselves. Likewise it was God who established the covenant of grace. It was not established by mutual agreement between God and man, not even with man's consent. The covenant came into being by a divine fiat. Said God in the garden: 'I will put enmity' (Gen. 3:15), and to Abraham he said: 'I will establish my covenant' (Gen. 17:7). Therefore it is far better to define the covenant as a disposition made by God in behalf of man than to describe it as an agreement between God and man. The New Testament word for *covenant* is *diathēkē*, not *sunthēkē*. The latter term designates an agreement between parties with equal rights, the former a disposition made by one in behalf of another as, for instance, a testament or will. However, in its execution the covenant has two parties. God does the promising and the commanding; man is under obligation to believe and to obey.

Election determines *who* are to be saved. The covenant of grace concerns the *manner* of their salvation. The elect are to be saved through faith in the Christ, who satisfied the divine penal justice by dying in their stead on the accursed cross, and by His perfect obedience to the divine law merited for them eternal righteousness. That is meant when it is said that Christ's 'passive' and 'active' obedience is the ground of their salvation. On that ground alone they rest in faith. By faith they appropriate to themselves Christ and all His saving benefits.

Election was wholly unconditional. It was not conditioned on man's faith and obedience. God did not choose sinners to eternal life *if* they should believe and obey. Nor did He choose certain persons to eternal life because He foreknew that they would believe and obey. The covenant of grace, on the other hand, is both conditional and unconditional. Salvation is conditioned on faith and obedience. Only those who believe in Christ as Saviour and honour Him as Lord will be saved. However, those conditions are met by the sovereign grace of God. Before faith and obedience become acts of man they are gifts of God. The Bible says: 'By grace are ye saved through faith; and that not of yourselves; it is the gift of God', and 'We are his workmanship, created in Christ Jesus for good works, which God afore prepared that we should walk in them' (Eph. 2:8, 10 ASV).

Occasionally one hears it said that, while election stresses divine sovereignty, the covenant stresses human responsibility. That statement suffers from over-simplification. Admittedly, however, it does contain a modicum of truth. It would be more precise to say that, while divine sovereignty is stressed strongly in the doctrine of election, and human responsibility is implicit in it, divine sovereignty is stressed no less strongly in the doctrine of the covenant, and human responsibility is explicit in it. In the covenant of grace God most explicitly demands faith and obedience. He holds man emphatically and unqualifiedly accountable for the exercise of faith and the rendering of obedience.

It would hardly be correct to say that in election God regarded His own as so many individuals only, and not as an organism. They are 'a chosen generation' (I Peter 2:9). Yet, it may be asserted that in the covenant the organic unity of God's people receives greater emphasis. While election stresses the fact that God chose one of twin brothers, Jacob, not Esau (Rom 9:10-12), the doctrine of the covenant stresses the truth that in imparting saving grace to men, God, although not bound by family ties, graciously takes them into account. He established the covenant with Abraham and his seed after him in their generations, to be a God unto him and to his seed after him (Gen. 17:7).

As was previously stated, election was in a real sense universal. Although God did not decree the salvation of all men, He has His elect in every nation and in every period of human history. Yet, it must be granted that the note of universalism is fully as prominent in the doctrine of the covenant as in that of election. Election spells the salvation of some, not all. The covenant of grace spells the salvation, not, to be sure, of every individual, yet of the human race, the world. Christ is in very deed 'the Saviour of the world' (I John 4:14).

It has become evident that in numerous ways the Scriptural teaching of the covenant of grace complements the Scriptural teaching of divine election. From that fact significant deductions may be made as to the bearing of the covenant on evangelism. Following are some of those deductions, each of them Biblical.

The Actualization of Election

God chose His own from everlasting. In eternity He decreed that they would be saved. Likewise in eternity He decreed the entire method and all the means of their salvation. However, the actual salvation of the elect by that method and those means takes place in time. Now precisely that is subsumed under the term *covenant of grace*.

In order that the elect might be saved, the Son of God had to become incarnate. As the Mediator between God and man He had to endure the wrath of God against the sin of man and to render to God that perfect obedience which the first Adam had failed to render. He did all that and thus merited eternal life for the elect. However, their salvation was not thus actualized. They have to be told of the saving work of Christ. That is done in the gospel. And, having heard the gospel, they must trust in Christ as Saviour and serve Him as Lord. That is accomplished through the gracious application of the evangel to their hearts by the Holy Spirit. Only then are they saved. In fine, their salvation is realized by way of the covenant of grace.

It is apparent, then, that the preaching of the gospel is an important link in the chain of events that constitute the realization of election. And not only is it an important link; it is a necessary one. The elect who die in infancy and elect imbeciles aside, all of God's elect are saved through the gospel; not one of them is saved without the evangel. 'How shall they call on him in whom they have not believed? and how shall they believe in him of whom they have not heard? and how shall they hear without a preacher?' (Rom. 10:14).

In the foregoing chapter it was said repeatedly and emphatically that election demands evangelism. Now it must be asserted just as emphatically that evangelism is indispensable in the actualization of the salvation of God's elect. And that is a way of saying that the covenant of grace and evangelism are inseparable. *Evangelism is inherent in the covenant of grace.*

Separation unto Universalism

When God was about to establish the covenant of grace with Abraham, He separated him, together with his descendants, from the peoples of the earth. God commanded him: 'Get thee out of thy country, and from thy kindred, and from thy father's house, unto a land that I will show thee' (Gen. 12:1). Early in history God thus drew a sharp line of demarcation between His covenant people and the world. And, let it be said at once, that line God will never permit men to erase. It will continue throughout time and extend even into eternity. The antithesis of God's friends and God's enemies is everlasting.

However, that is by no means the whole story. God went on to say to Abraham: 'And I will make of thee a great nation, and I will bless thee, and make thy name great; and thou shalt be a blessing. And I will bless them that bless thee, and curse him that curseth thee: and in thee shall all families of the earth be blessed' (Gen. 12:2, 3). How clear that the separation of Abraham and his descendants was not an end in itself! It was but a means to an end. The end was that in them all nations should be blessed. The end was universalism.

The same lesson is implicit in the prophecies of that mysterious character Balaam. Although he was God's enemy, yet it pleased God to put His words into Balaam's mouth. Looking down from the top of the rocks on the children of Israel encamped in the valley below, the son of Beor spoke: 'The people shall dwell alone, and shall not be reckoned among the nations' (Num. 23:9). But in his final benediction he uttered the Messianic prophecy: 'There shall come a Star out of Jacob, and a Sceptre shall rise out of Israel, and shall smite the corners of Moab, and destroy all the children of Sheth. And Edom shall be a possession, Seir also shall be a possession for his enemies; and Israel shall do valiantly. Out of Jacob shall come he that shall have dominion' (Num. 24:17–19).

Planted by God in the land of Canaan, God's chosen people resembled a hedged vineyard. To the west it was protected by the Great Sea; to the north it was locked in by the mountainous region of Hermon and Lebanon; to the east and the south it was enclosed by expansive deserts. To an extent Israel was geographically isolated. And yet Palestine proved to be ideally situated as a focus of widespread influence. It was located on the Mediterranean Sea, which, as its very name indicates, was the centre of the ancient world. It lay at the crossroads of three continents: Asia, Africa, and Europe. A more strategic spot could hardly have been found from which the light of the gospel might shine out to the nations and the warmth of Christianity might radiate to all peoples.

It has often been said that ancient Israel was *isolated* from the world. But it would be far better to speak of Israel's *insulation*. Its isolation, such as it was, served as a means to the end of universalism. As a wire is wont to be insulated in order that the electric current which it carries may reach its intended destination instead of being lost in short circuits, so God's chosen people was separated from the pagan peoples of the earth in order that in the fullness of time it might bring forth the Saviour of the world and proclaim His evangel to the ends of the earth.

In the present dispensation, too, separation is a means to the end of universalism. The New Testament is replete with exhortations to the church to come out of the world. The very word which is used most frequently to designate the church, *ekklēsia*, describes it as a congregation which has been *called out*. Yet, addressing the members of His church, the Saviour said: 'Ye are the salt of the earth', and 'Ye are the light of the world' (Matt. 5:13,14). And He appointed them to be His witnesses 'unto the uttermost part of the earth' (Acts 1:8).

The truth that separation is unto universalism has often been neglected. There have been churches which stressed separation to the neglect of universalism. Even today, in this age of missions, there are such churches. They would prevent the world from invading the church, but they also keep the church from invading the world. Perhaps they insist that only the pure Word of God be preached from their pulpits, but they fail to proclaim the true gospel to the lost. They would build up saints in the faith, but they do not seek to persuade the unsaved to faith. Priding themselves on their orthodoxy, they are afflicted with orthodoxism. Such churches are slumbering. If they do not awake and give heed to the clarion voice of the church's King, bidding them proclaim the evangel to those without, sooner or later they will be sleeping the sleep of death.

On the other hand, the truth that separation is unto universalism is often distorted. More than a few churches stress universalism at the expense of separation. Strange though it may seem, they are more intent on bringing the gospel to the world than on keeping worldliness out of the church. They send out missionaries in considerable numbers to the heathen, but all the time the cancer of worldliness is spreading through their members, and nothing is done about it. But a worldly church cannot long continue active in truly Christian missions. Invariably corruption of the gospel message goes hand in hand with conformity to the world. Unless they repent, such churches are sure to degenerate into synagogues of Satan.

Covenant Children and Aliens

The children of believers as well as their parents are included in God's gracious covenant. That is a clear teaching of Scripture, and a prominent one. God established His covenant with Abraham and his seed (Gen. 17:7). And in his Pentecostal sermon Peter said to a predominantly Jewish audience: 'The promise is unto you and your children' (Acts 2:39).

However, the continuation of the covenant from generation to generation is not automatic. Children do not inherit saving grace from their believing parents as they may inherit a piece of real estate. Nor is continuation without exception. Some children of believers become covenantbreakers. In the continuation of His covenant from parents to children God is wont to employ means. The means is Christian education. Only if Christian parents train up a child in the way he should go, have they the right to expect that he will not depart from it when he is old (Prov. 22:6).

Strange to say, there are professing Christians who largely, if not completely, neglect the religious education of their children. They fail to provide such instruction for them either in the home or in the church, and it does not occur to them to enrol their children in a Christian day-school. Yet, equally strange to say, they have an apparent zeal for evangelism. Such parents resemble a couple which clothe and feed the children of their needy neighbours but neglect to provide the necessities of life for their own household. To change the simile, they are like a general who invades a foreign country without keeping strong his base of operations in his own land. If all Christian parents should follow their example, there soon would be no missionaries to send out to other peoples.

On the other hand, there are also believers who concentrate on the training of covenant children to such an extent that they take little or no interest in evangelizing those who are as yet 'without Christ, being aliens from the commonwealth of Israel, and strangers from the covenants of promise, having no hope, and without God in the world' (Eph. 2:12). That, too, is most reprehensible. And it is rooted in too restricted a view of the covenant of grace.

God has His elect in every land and in every age, and He knows them all. He has given them to the Son, who will see to it that not one of them perishes. Christ counts them among His sheep, for He said to His earliest disciples: 'Other sheep I have, which are not of this fold:

them also I must bring, and they shall hear my voice; and there shall be one fold and one shepherd' (John 10:16). Because God counts them with His people, He encouraged His servant Paul in apparently God-forsaken Corinth: 'Be not afraid, but speak, and hold not thy peace . . . for I have much people in this city' (Acts 18:9, 10). In his Pentecostal sermon Peter informed his Jewish hearers that the promise was not only unto them and their children, but 'to all that are afar off, even as many as the Lord our God shall call' (Acts 2:39). Throughout the centuries God has been mindful of His promise, 'It shall come to pass, that in the place where it was said unto them, Ye are not my people, there it shall be said unto them, Ye are the sons of the living God' (Hos. 1:10; Rom. 9:26). That promise still holds. And the Lord Jesus coupled with a severe warning to covenant children a blessed promise for aliens and strangers when He said: 'Many shall come from the east and west, and shall sit down with Abraham and Isaac and Jacob in the kingdom of heaven. But the children of the kingdom shall be cast out into outer darkness: there shall be weeping and gnashing of teeth' (Matt. 8:11, 12).

How clear that the sweeping statement can stand: wherever the evangel is, there is the covenant! The church is indeed the blessed recipient of God's covenant mercies, but it is also the God-appointed responsible agent for the extension of those mercies to others. That, as well as the training of covenant children, is its *covenantal duty*.

The Convert and His House

When the jailer at Philippi inquired what he had to do in order to be saved, Paul and Silas replied: 'Believe on the

Lord Jesus Christ, and thou shalt be saved, and thy house' (Acts 16:31).

What did they mean when they told the jailer that, in case he believed, his house, as well as he himself, would be saved? They must have had in mind one of the most comforting aspects of the covenant of grace: that God has promised to be the God, not only of those who believe, but also of their seed, and that, hence, He is wont as a general rule to bestow saving grace on the children of believers.

What an inducement for seeking souls, like the jailer, to embrace the gospel! Their faith will entail, in addition to their own salvation, the salvation of those who are nearest and dearest to them, their children, and even generations to come.

And what encouragement he who brings the gospel to the unsaved may draw from the same teaching of Holy Writ! Not only may he rest assured that God has His people, and Christ His sheep, in the most unlikely places and that every one of them is sure to respond sooner or later to the gospel in faith; he also has the assurance that, when God begins the good work in the heart of a father or mother, He will, by and large, continue that work in the hearts of their children; yes, will impart saving grace to children's children unto distant generations. Thus each conversion may be expected to lead to countless conversions, and the seed of the gospel that is sown today may well continue to bring forth fruit, abundant fruit, for centuries and even millennia.

5: God's Sovereign Commission and Evangelism

A SEMINARY STUDENT WAS TO PREPARE FOR 'practice preaching' a sermon on the text, 'Thy will be done in earth, as it is in heaven' (Matt. 6:10). After making some study of the text, he consulted with the instructor. Said the student: 'I have come to the conclusion that this petition of the Lord's Prayer speaks of God's revealed or preceptive will, not of his secret or decretive will.' When the instructor ventured the opinion that he might be right, the student asked: 'May I, then, conclude that the text has nothing to do with divine sovereignty?' The answer could only be that now he was badly mistaken.

The notion that the sovereignty of God comes to expression only in the divine decrees is rather widespread, but exceedingly erroneous. God's sovereignty comes to expression also in the divine commands.

That being the case, human responsibility is but a corollary of divine sovereignty. God commands sovereignly and for that very reason must be obeyed. Therefore, by all the rules of sound logic he who most strongly stresses the sovereignty of God must also stress most strongly the responsibility of man.

Attention may here be called to a curious misunderstanding of the Reformed theology. It has often been said that, while Calvinism excels in emphasis on divine sovereignty, Arminianism excels in emphasis on human responsibility. A worse caricature of Calvinism is hardly imaginable. Admittedly, there have been self-styled Calvinists who belittle human responsibility, but the reason for their doing so lay in their inconsistency. Calvinism is not so inconsistent. Precisely because it stresses divine sovereignty strongly, it stresses human responsibility no less strongly. And is it not obvious that the Reformed theology as a matter of fact stresses human responsibility not less strongly, but more so, than does Arminian theology? Arminianism teaches that God adjusts His commands to the enfeebled powers of man and therefore never demands of man what he cannot do; the Reformed faith holds that God requires of man perfect obedience to His law even though man in his fallen state is incapable of rendering such obedience. Arminianism tells us that human responsibility is limited by human inability; the Reformed faith recognizes no such restriction.

To apply the foregoing to evangelism, the sovereignty of God comes to vigorous expression in the many missionary commands of the Bible, and in the measure in which one recognizes the divine sovereignty, in that very measure must one be zealous in carrying out those commands.

Christ's Mediatorial Sovereignty

Christ is God and as such is sovereign. Sovereignty belongs alike to each of the three persons of the Godhead.

Sovereignty belongs to Christ in another sense also. When He died on Calvary's cross, a most important part of His mediatorial work had been accomplished. By what theologians are wont to term His passive and active obedience, He had fully merited salvation for those whom the Father had given Him. Therefore, shortly before bowing His head in death, He exclaimed: 'It is finished' (John 19:30). For His finished work He was rewarded by the Father with mediatorial royalty. Because He had become obedient unto death, even the death of the cross, God highly exalted Him and gave Him a name which is above every name (Phil. 2:8, 9). Henceforth He was 'the head over all things' (Eph. 1:22). Now He could rightly put forth the stupendous claim, 'All authority hath been given unto me in heaven and on earth' (Matt. 28:18 ASV). Significantly, He prefaced the Great Commission with that claim. That makes the Great Commission an assertion of Christ's mediatorial sovereignty.

During His public ministry Christ sent forth the twelve and the seventy to preach the gospel, as well as to heal the sick, but expressly commanded them to restrict their evangelistic activity to 'the lost sheep of the house of Israel' (Matt. 10:6). His death and resurrection brought about a radical change. Those events mark the transition from the relative nationalism of the old dispensation to the unrestricted universalism of the new. In His appearances to His followers the risen Christ repeatedly issued the command to evangelize the world. At Jerusalem He instructed them: 'Thus it is written, and thus it behoved Christ to suffer, and to rise from the dead the third day: and that repentance and remission of sins should be preached in his name among all nations, beginning at Jerusalem. And ye are witnesses of these things' (Luke 24:46-48). When the eleven met the Lord by appointment on a mountain in Galilee, He gave them what has come to be known as the Great Commission (Matt. 28:18-20). And just before His ascension into heaven from mount Olivet He foretold: 'Ye shall receive power after that the Holy Ghost is come upon you: and ye shall be witnesses unto me both in Jerusalem and in Judea, and in Samaria, and unto the uttermost part of the earth' (Acts 1:8).

Here a most significant observation must be made. As was said, Christ's death and resurrection mark the transition from nationalism to universalism. But let it be noted well, precisely the same events spell also the coronation of Christ the Mediator. That transition and that coronation were not unrelated, although simultaneous, events. They occurred simultaneously because they were one and the same event. Christ was crowned in order that 'at the name of Jesus every knee should bow, of things in heaven, and things in earth, and things under the earth; and that every tongue should confess that Jesus Christ is Lord' (Phil. 2: 10, 11), all of which was to be brought about by the universal proclamation of His gospel. In royal majesty Christ declared to His apostles: 'As my Father hath sent me, even so send I you' (John 20: 21). It was the sovereign Christ who sovereignly charged His church with the Great Commission, 'All authority hath been given unto me in heaven and on earth. Go ye therefore, and make disciples of all the nations, baptizing them into the name of the Father, and of the Son, and of the Holy Spirit: teaching them to observe all things whatsoever I commanded you: and lo, I am with you always, even unto the end of the world' (Matt. 28: 18–20 ASV).

The Abiding Validity of the Great Commission

It has been suggested that, after the outpouring of the Holy Spirit, the New Testament church has little, if indeed any, need of the Great Commission. Having received the Holy Spirit, the church is said to witness for Christ willingly, freely, spontaneously, not under the external compulsion of a commandment. For the believer of the new dispensation, witnessing is said to be as natural as breathing. As birds take to flying and fishes to swimming, so the Christian is said to take to witnessing.

That the outpouring of the Spirit at Pentecost rendered the church a witnessing church must be readily granted not only, but strongly stressed. Jesus declared it in so many words when He promised power from on high to the eleven men who constituted the nucleus of His church. Said He: 'And ye shall be witnesses unto me' (Acts 1:8). It is true also that witnessing is the essence of Christianity. Where witnessing is lacking, there Christianity is lacking. Did not Jesus assert: 'Whosoever shall deny me before men, him will I also deny before my Father which is in heaven' (Matt. 10:33)? However, to conclude that the Christian church and the individual Christian have outgrown the need for Scriptural commands to witness, the Great Commission included, is quite unwarranted.

That conclusion has dispensational implications. Granted that the old dispensation and the new are characterized by significant differences of emphasis, to place them over against each other as the dispensation of law and that of the Spirit is unscriptural. David's prayer, 'Take not thy Holy Spirit from me' (Ps. 51:11), plainly indicates that he had experienced the renewing influence of the Spirit. And the New Testament, the epistles as well as the gospels, teem with commands for Christian living.

The position under discussion also savours of perfectionism. The best Christian is still a poor Christian. No believer is yielded completely to the influence of the Spirit of God. Every one of us must frequently confess: 'The good that I would I do not; but the evil which I would not, that I do' (Rom. 7:19). There is not a believer who has never remained silent when he should have confessed his Lord. There is not one of us but has had cause to weep bitterly after the manner of Simon Peter and for the same reason (Matt. 26:75). We all need to be reminded of the first and great commandment of the law, 'Thou shalt love the Lord thy God, with all thy heart, and with all thy soul, and with all thy mind' (Matt. 22:37). And not one of us has progressed in sanctification to the point that he has no more need for the commandment to witness for his Lord and Saviour. We do not love Him nearly as dearly as we ought. And when we are most fully yielded to the gracious influence of the Holy Spirit and our hearts burn with love for Him who first loved us, instead of declaring our independence of the divine law, we exult: 'I delight in the law of God after the inward man' (Rom. 7:22).

Universal Recognition of Christ's Sovereignty

In the Great Commission the sovereign Christ charged His disciples with *teaching*. He would have men everywhere *taught*. The duty of *teaching* looms exceedingly large.

According to the Authorized Version the command to teach occurs twice in the Great Commission. It says: 'Go ye therefore, and teach all nations . . . teaching them to observe all things whatsoever I have commanded you.' While the translation of the American Standard Version, 'Make disciples of all the nations', and the almost identical translation of the Revised Standard Version are to be preferred to the translation 'Teach all nations', these two renderings are not far apart. The word *disciple* is derived from a Latin verb which means *to learn*. A disciple, then, is a learner, and obviously a learner presupposes a teacher. It must also be noted that all three of the aforenamed versions employ the word *teaching* in the latter part of the passage.

It follows that the notion must be rejected that in evangelism men are first to be induced by other means than teaching, for instance by a strong emotional appeal, to become disciples, and are subsequently to be taught. To be sure, teaching need not be unemotional, and all of Christ's disciples must be taught so long as they live. But the point is that men are to be made disciples by being taught the Word of God.

The notion must also be rejected that men must first be made disciples and, that having been accomplished, must then be taught to observe Christ's commandments. If Christ had meant that, He would have said: 'Make disciples of all the nations *and* teach them to observe all things whatsoever I have commanded you.' Rather are men to be made Christ's disciples *by* being taught to observe Christ's commandments. Instructing them to keep those commandments is the method by which they are to be rendered disciples.

Now that amounts to saying that the keeping of Christ's commandments is part and parcel of discipleship. This truth deserves much emphasis. One becomes a disciple of the Christ, not merely by receiving Him in faith as Saviour, but by also acknowledging Him as Lord. Those two acts are inseparable. Faith in Christ and obedience to Him are, as it were, the two sides of one coin. Small wonder that in the New Testament the same word which in some contexts means *to believe*, in other contexts is correctly rendered *to obey*. In Acts 28:24 it is said that, in response to Paul's preaching to the Jews at Rome, 'some *believed* the things that were spoken, and some believed not'. In Galatians 5:7 Paul puts the reproving question: 'Who did hinder you that ye should not *obey* the truth?' In both passages the identical Greek verb occurs.

Thus it becomes apparent that the Great Commission

is a statement of the aim of evangelism. It is that all nations may observe Christ's commandments and, in so doing, may acknowledge His sovereignty. The end of evangelism is the universal recognition of the sovereignty of Christ.

Reliance on Christ's Sovereignty

The disciples must have been shocked when the Lord commissioned them to make disciples of all the nations. That assignment was nothing short of overwhelming. It was a case of eleven men against the world, of eleven relatively ignorant men of the most despised nation under the sun against all the power and wisdom of the world. That feeble, by human standards utterly negligible, band was given orders to conquer the glory that was Greece and the grandeur and might of the world-spanning Roman empire, together with whatever wild tribes might be dwelling beyond Caesar's domain.

'Impossible!' they thought. 'Utterly impossible!' they reasoned. 'Unthinkable!' they felt.

Their Commander knew their thoughts. But His thoughts were higher, infinitely higher. Said He in effect: 'Did you in your own strength confide, your striving would indeed be losing. But remember that you are not alone. I, the man of God's own choosing, am on your side. Lord Sabaoth is My name. Mine are all authority and all power on earth and in heaven. Yes, even Satan and all his host cannot so much as stir without My permission. To be sure, in the world you will have tribulation; but fear not, for I have overcome the world (John 16:33). Apart from Me you can do nothing (John 15:5), but by the strength which I will supply you can do all things (Phil. 4:13). In Me your labour will not be in vain (I Cor. 15:58). Through the operation of My sovereign grace in the hearts of men there will be numerous converts for you to baptize into the name of the Father, the Son, and the Holy Spirit, thus to signify and to seal unto them salvation by the Triune God and fellowship with Him in the communion of His church. And, although the task assigned to you will not be finished during your lifetime, be not discouraged. My church, against which the very gates of hell cannot prevail (Matt. 16:18), will carry on. As I am with you, so will I be with it to the end of time. The very works of the devil I will overrule so that they redound to the consummation of My kingdom. The blood of martyrs I will render the seed of the church. When earth's potentates close the doors of many nations to prevent the evangel from entering, I will see to it that the message of salvation penetrates gates of brass and iron curtains. Though preachers of the gospel may be bound, My Word will never be bound (II Tim. 2:9). And when time shall be no more, great voices in heaven will sing: "The kingdoms of this world are become the kingdoms of our Lord and of his Christ; and he shall reign for ever and ever" (Rev. 11:15).'

The Great Commission is usually thought of as a missionary command. It is that and far more than that. Its theme is *The Sovereign Christ*. It is a glorious declaration of His sovereignty. It is a sovereign command to proclaim Him to all nations. It is an unqualified demand for universal recognition of His sovereignty. It is a cordial invitation to complete reliance on His sovereignty. It is a sure prophecy of the consummation of His sovereignty.

> Jesus shall reign where'er the sun
> Does his successive journeys run;
> His kingdom stretch from shore to shore,
> Till moons shall wax and wane no more.

6: God and the Scope of Evangelism

IN RELIGIOUS CIRCLES MUCH IS BEING SAID about universalism. The universal fatherhood of God, the universal brotherhood of man, universal peace, and universal salvation are favourite topics. Most of that talk comes from modernist quarters and therefore is, to say the least, suspect for believers. Some of it is definitely anti-Christian. However, let no one jump to the conclusion that there is no such thing as Christian universalism. There most certainly is. Christianity is a universal religion and demands universal evangelism.

Universalism in the Old Dispensation

The old dispensation and the new are customarily distinguished as the dispensation of nationalism and that of universalism. By and large, that distinction is valid. Israel was God's peculiar people. Moses said to the nation: 'Thou art an holy people unto the Lord thy God: the Lord thy God hath chosen thee to be a special people unto himself, above all people that are upon the face of the earth' (Deut. 7:6). The Psalmist sang: 'He showeth his word unto Jacob, his statutes and his judgments unto Israel. He hath not dealt so with any nation: and as for his judgments, they have not known them. Praise ye the Lord' (Ps. 147:19, 20). On the other hand, at the very beginning of the new dispensation the church was commissioned and empowered to bring the gospel to all the nations.

However, let no one harbour the thought that the nationalism of the old dispensation was absolute. To suppose that, would be a most serious error. Nothing of the kind was the case.

The reason is supremely significant. The Old Testament as well as the New is God's self-revelation. The God revealed in both is the same. To be sure, there is progress in His revelation of Himself, but there is no contradiction whatever. Augustine was right when he said that the New Testament is latent in the Old, the Old patent in the New.

Now obviously, the God of the New Testament is the God of all the earth and of all nations. Said Peter, when God called him to baptize a Roman centurion: 'Of a truth I perceive that God is no respecter of persons; but in every nation he that feareth him and worketh righteousness is accepted with him' (Acts 10:34, 35). It is just as obvious that the God of the Old Testament is the God of all peoples. The notion that Jehovah was a mere tribal, or at most a national, God is a figment of man's imagination, completely foreign to the Old Testament. He created the human race. He promised a Saviour to the fallen human race. Through His servant Noah He warned the ungodly human race of impending judgment. By saving Noah and his family from the deluge He preserved the human race. When He set Abraham apart as the progenitor of His chosen people, He promised that in him all families of the earth would be blessed.

Again, no one can dispute that the God of the New Testament claims to be the only true and living God. Paul wrote to the believers in idolatrous Corinth: 'Though there be that are called gods . . . to us there is but one God, the Father, of whom are all things, and we in him' (I Cor. 8:5, 6). It is just as indisputable that the God of the Old Testament makes the identical claim. In fact, no truth stands out more prominently in the Old Testament. Moses' pronouncement, 'Hear, O Israel; the Lord our God is one Lord' (Deut. 6:4), is its keynote. The refrain, 'Thou art God alone' (Ps. 86:10), peals forth from all its pages.

Because He is the God of all the earth and the one and only God, the God of the Old Testament cannot but demand universal recognition and allegiance. All that is explicit in His call, 'Look unto me, and be ye saved, all the ends of the earth; for I am God, and there is none else' (Isa. 45:22).

Thus it was that the God of Israel commanded His servant Jonah to preach repentance to the wicked inhabitants of Nineveh, capital of the Assyrian empire, and, when they turned from their iniquities, 'repented of the evil that he had said he would do unto them; and he did it not' (Jonah 3:10).

It is no exaggeration to say that the Old Testament teems with prophecies of coming universalism. The recital of them all would fill many pages. Familiar are Psalm 72:8, 'He shall have dominion also from sea to sea, and from the river unto the ends of the earth'; Psalm 86:9, 'All nations whom thou hast made shall come and worship before thee, O Lord, and shall glorify thy name'; Psalm 87:4, 'I will make mention of Rahab and Babylon to them that know me: behold Philistia, and Tyre, with Ethiopia; this man was born there.' The prophet Joel foretold the events of Pentecost. God spoke by him: 'It shall come to pass afterward, that I will pour out my Spirit upon all flesh' (Joel 2:28). Beyond all doubt, Daniel's interpretation of Nebuchadnezzar's dream image had the strongest Messianic overtones. Speaking of the stone, cut out without hands, which smote the image of gold, silver, brass, iron, and a combination of iron and clay, demolished it, and itself became a great mountain that filled the earth, the prophet said: 'In the days of these kings shall the God of heaven set up a kingdom which shall never be destroyed; and the kingdom shall not be left to other people, but it shall break in pieces and consume all these kingdoms, and it shall stand for ever' (Dan. 2:44).

Certain parables of the Lord Jesus must also be mentioned here, for they, too, were spoken before the new dispensation was ushered in. He concluded the parable of the unfaithful husbandmen by telling the Jewish religious leaders of His day that the kingdom of God would be taken from them and given to a nation bringing forth the fruits thereof (Matt. 21:43). And in the parable of the supper He taught that, when those who were bidden would refuse to come, the poor, the maimed, the halt, and the blind from the streets and lanes of the city, as well as from the highways and hedges, would be invited to take their places and would even be compelled to come in (Luke 14:16–24).

Even more arresting is the fact that in the old dispensation there were actual anticipations of the universalism of the new. Rahab of Jericho (Josh. 6:17–25; Heb. 11:31; James 2:25), Ruth the Moabitess (Book of Ruth; Matt. 1:5), Naaman the Syrian (II Kings 5; Luke 4:27), the magi from the east (Matt. 2:1–12), and the Samaritan woman (John 4) are outstanding examples. All of these became believers.

Christ's Birth and Universalism

It would not be correct to assert that the dispensation of universalism commenced at the birth of the Son of God. Had that been the case, He would not have restricted the evangelistic activity of His first disciples to Israel (Matt.

10:6). As will be shown presently, universalism was ushered in by Christ's death. And yet, His birth made universalism a foregone conclusion. That is implicit in the Scriptural teaching that He was born in 'the fulness of the time' (Gal. 4:4).

God had foreordained from eternity the exact time of the coming of His Son in the flesh. He had also foreordained the world scene at that time. And in His providence, which is nothing else than the working out of His eternal plan, He saw to it that that scene was most favourable for the spread of the gospel.

Providentially, the city on the yellow Tiber was now the capital of humanity. Not only had the Romans built numerous roads which made travel from one land to another possible, they had also by the common grace of God provided a goodly measure of law and order throughout the world. On more occasions than one Paul's Roman citizenship stood him in good stead on his missionary journeys (cf. Acts 16:36-40; 22:24-29; 25:9-12).

God, in whose hand is the king's heart as the rivers of water and who turns it whithersoever He wills (Prov. 21:1), put it into the heart of Alexander the Great to make Greek the language of literature the world over. That accounts for it that the New Testament, although authored largely by Jews, was written in Greek. A common language could not but prove a great boon to the evangelization of the nations.

Again, it was God who had dispersed Israel among the nations. Wherever the Jews went, they carried with them their Bible, the Old Testament, with all its Messianic prophecies and promises. That, no doubt, was a factor contributing to an expectation, even in the gentile world, of a coming Messiah. Such Roman writers as Virgil, Suetonius, and Tacitus called attention to an ancient prediction that, the last days having come, the Son of God would descend from heaven to destroy the serpent and to establish a golden age, and that, with Judaea as its centre, a world-empire would be founded.

Jesus was born on the very threshold of the dispensation of universalism.

Christ's Death and Universalism

All the light of sacred story gathers around the cross of Christ. The whole of human history centres about His cross. The cross marks the end of the old dispensation, the beginning of the new.

That is easily demonstrated from the Word of God. The old dispensation was that of shadows; the new is that of truth, in the sense of reality. The ceremonial law, particularly as it concerned bloody sacrifices, foreshadowed the shedding of Christ's sacrificial blood on Calvary. Therefore by His death Christ abolished the law of ceremonies. At the very moment when He gave up the ghost, 'the veil of the temple was rent in twain from the top to the bottom' (Mark 15:37, 38). The veil separated the holiest place of all from the holy place. In the holiest place stood the ark, covered by the mercy seat, over which hovered the shekinah, the visible majesty of the divine presence, and the cherubim with outspread wings. Only once a year, on the great day of atonement, one man, the high priest, was permitted to pass through the veil into the presence of God; and even he might not enter without blood, to be sprinkled by him upon the mercy seat in order to make atonement for his own sins and the sins of the people (Lev. 16:1–17). Now that Christ's lifeblood had been shed, God tore the veil in two, signifying that the ceremonial law was nullified and that henceforth every believer in Christ might, without the mediation of a holy place, a human priest, or a sacrifice for sin, come boldly to the divine throne of grace. How clear that the death of Christ terminated the old dispensation and initiated the new!

The Bible teaches specifically that the death of Christ marked the end of the dispensation of nationalism and the beginning of the dispensation of universalism. When certain Greeks, not Greek Jews but gentiles, expressed a desire to see Him, the Saviour, deeply moved, exclaimed: 'Verily, verily, I say unto you, Except a corn of wheat fall into the ground and die, it abideth alone: but if it die, it bringeth forth much fruit', and referring to the manner of his death, namely crucifixion: 'I, if I be lifted up from the earth, will draw all men unto me' (John 12: 24, 32). And Paul told the gentile believers at Ephesus that they, who once were far off, were made nigh by the blood of Christ and that Christ had reconciled both Jews and gentiles unto God in one body by the cross (Eph. 2: 13, 16).

Christ having died, and the Father having put the stamp of approval on His finished work by raising Him from the dead, the stage was now set for the giving of the Great Commission and the outpouring of the Holy Spirit, by which the church was empowered to carry the gospel to the ends of the earth.

If Christ's death spells universalism, then that death may well be the central theme of the universally proclaimed evangel. So it is. The great missionary apostle wrote to the church at Corinth: 'We preach Christ crucified' (I Cor. 1: 23), and 'I determined not to know anything among you, save Jesus Christ, and him crucified' (I Cor. 2: 2).

Christ's Exaltation and Evangelism

In the foregoing chapter much was said concerning the bearing of Christ's exaltation on world-wide evangelism. Brevity is now in order.

By raising Him from the dead. God the Father expressed His full approval of the Son's finished mediatorial labours. And so it is nothing strange that the same apostle who was determined to know nothing save Jesus Christ and Him crucified, made the resurrection the burden of his preaching. Christ's death and resurrection constitute one theme.

Through suffering Christ entered into His glory (Luke 24:26). As reward for obediently pouring out His soul unto death, the Father divided Him a portion with the great, He divided the spoil with the strong (Isa. 53:12), and God highly exalted Him, giving Him a name which is above every name, that at the name of Jesus every knee should bow, and every tongue should confess Him to be Lord (Phil. 2:9–11). That was the meaning of His resurrection from the dead and His session at the Father's right hand. No wonder that the risen and ascending Christ commanded the universal proclamation of His gospel!

Not only did the glorified Christ require of His disciples universal evangelism, it was He who, by the right hand of God exalted, poured out upon His church the Holy Spirit, thus enabling it to witness for Him to all the nations (Acts 2:33).

The same almighty King will be with His church, protecting and prospering it, in the proclamation of the evangel until the day dawns when the earth shall be full of the knowledge of the Lord as the waters cover the sea (Isa. 11:9).

Christ's exaltation demands universal evangelism. His

gospel must be proclaimed everywhere, both because He is the universal king and in order that He may be recognized as such universally.

Pentecost and Universalism

Pentecost is often spoken of as the birthday of the Christian church. That is a mistake. Ever since the fall of man there has been but one way of salvation. All who were saved were saved by faith in Christ. And all who believed in Him were members of His body, the church. As regards salvation, the only difference between the saints of the old dispensation and those of the new is that the former were saved by faith in the Christ of prophecy, whereas the latter are saved by faith in the Christ of history. But it goes without saying that the Christ of prophecy and the Christ of history are one and the same. It follows that, if Adam and Eve believed the protevangelium of Genesis 3:15, as presumably they did, they became the first members of Christ's church. And Abel, Abraham, David, and Isaiah were members of the Christian church as well as were Peter, Paul, Augustine, and Luther.

Although Pentecost was not the birthday of the Christian church, it does mark a most significant turning point in the history of the church. The outpouring of the Holy Spirit upon the church implemented the transition from nationalism to universalism.

Observe what transpired at Pentecost!

The disciples of Jesus were gathered in one place. They were under orders to make disciples of all the nations of the earth. But they were few, very few. And they were feeble, exceedingly feeble. Had they relied on their own strength, their striving could have resulted only in failure.

In fact, so weak were they that it did not so much as occur to them to pit their strength against that of the world. They had no strength, and they knew it. Yet the task of world conquest stared them in the face. Suddenly, miraculously, their Lord, at the right hand of God, came to their aid. He gave them power from on high, as He had promised. They heard 'a sound from heaven as of a rushing mighty wind, and it filled all the house where they were sitting'. Besides, 'there appeared unto them cloven tongues like as of fire, and it sat upon each of them' (Acts 2:2, 3). Two of the greatest forces of nature were unleashed, and these forces symbolized the almighty, irresistible, power of God the Holy Spirit. Thus empowered, they were presently proclaiming the gospel in many languages to men 'out of every nation under heaven . . .' (Acts 2:4-6). The accomplishment of their apparently hopeless task was well under way.

Nor was that the whole story. The disciples at Jerusalem were Jews. Like all Jews, they harboured powerful prejudices against the gentile nations. When Jonah refused to warn the Ninevites, he acted not merely as an obstreperous individual, but rather as a typical Israelite. Priding themselves on being the people of the Lord, Israelites were wont to look down with proud disdain on other peoples. If Jesus' disciples were to make disciples of all the nations, they would have to overcome that prejudice. They must have felt that, and they could hardly have helped wondering how that might be done; in fact, whether it could be done at all. But in the twinkling of an eye the Spirit of God swept that prejudice away. Before they fully realized what they were about, they found themselves preaching the gospel to 'proselytes', gentiles, as well as Jews (Acts 2:10).

But would their preaching bring results? That question

must have risen in their minds, for the Lord had commanded them, not merely to preach to the nations, but *to make disciples* of the nations. If they were troubled about that, as well they may have been, their worries were soon dispelled. Before the day was over, some three thousand souls were brought to repentance and faith in Christ through the irresistible application of the gospel by the Holy Spirit (Acts 2:41).

Thus the Jerusalem of Acts 2 became the counterpart of the Babel of Genesis 11. In both instances there was a miraculous display of divine power. The miracles were strikingly similar. Both at Babel and at Jerusalem God supernaturally caused men to speak in various tongues. But the consequences differed radically. At Babel there was confusion and division. Men were scattered abroad on all the face of the earth. That was the beginning of nationalism. At Jerusalem one message was proclaimed in many tongues. It was the evangel. By the Word of God, which is 'quick and powerful' (Heb. 4:12), the Spirit of God drew men from every nation under heaven into the one church of Christ. Pentecost spells both universalism and unity.

The outpouring of the Holy Spirit betokened the powerful implementation and the effective realization of Christian universalism.

Universalism and the Apostolic Church

It is difficult for gentile believers of this twentieth century to put themselves in the place of Jewish believers of the first century of the Christian era. So deeply had the truth that they of all nations of the earth were God's chosen people been branded upon their souls that it was well-nigh impossible for them to comprehend that the middle wall of partition between them and the gentiles had been broken down (Eph. 2:14) and that in Christ Jesus there was neither Jew nor Greek (Gal. 3:28).

For that reason, no doubt, God on various occasions forcefully reminded the apostolic church of its duty to preach the gospel to gentiles as well as Jews. At least four of those reminders are worthy of special note.

The evangelist Philip was led by the Spirit in a notably supernatural manner to bring the gospel to an Ethiopian of the court of Queen Candace. And the Spirit blessed Philip's message to the heart of this foreigner in such a way that he presently confessed Jesus Christ to be the Son of God and was baptized into membership of His body, the church (Acts 8:26-39).

In view of Peter's active participation in the events of Pentecost one might suppose that he was fully prepared henceforth to preach the gospel to any pagan anywhere. Yet such was by no means the case. He was in need of special instruction in order to be made willing to receive a Roman into the fellowship of believers. God gave him that instruction, again in a strikingly supernatural manner. On the housetop of Simon the tanner, at Joppa by the seaside, Peter, having fallen into a trance, saw a vessel descend from heaven. It contained all kinds of four-footed beasts, wild beasts, creeping things, and fowls. A voice from heaven commanded him to eat. When, mindful of the law which God Himself had given to the Jews, he refused to eat anything unclean, he was told: 'What God hath cleansed, that call not thou common.' In order that Peter might be fully assured of the will of God, this was done thrice. In obedience to the heavenly vision he presently preached the gospel to Cornelius and his household, and even before he had finished his sermon the Holy Spirit fell on his hearers.

[79]

His Jewish believing companions were astonished. But Peter judged that baptism should not be withheld from those who had received the Spirit. Gentiles though they were, they were baptized into the body of Christ (Acts 10).

But Peter was not God's chosen vessel to bear His name to the gentiles. Saul of Tarsus was that (Acts 9:15). As the gospel of the circumcision was committed to Peter, so was the gospel of the uncircumcision to Paul. And He that wrought effectually in Peter to the apostleship of the circumcision, the same was mighty in Paul toward the gentiles (Gal. 2:7, 8). Although 'a Hebrew of the Hebrews' (Phil. 3:5) – that is, the son of a Hebrew father and a Hebrew mother – Paul was born and reared in the province of Cilicia. By birth he was a Roman citizen, and he learned to know Greek culture as did none other of the apostles. His conversion, his calling by the Holy Spirit, his missionary journeys constitute the greater part of the story of universalism in the apostolic age. His labours in the evangel add up to the triumphant march of the gospel of Jesus Christ from Jerusalem, the capital of Jewry, to Rome, the capital of the world.

Acts 15 gives an account of what is commonly called the Council of Jerusalem. A grave problem was disturbing the peace of the early church. Among the Jewish believers were so-called Judaizers, who insisted that gentiles should be permitted to enter the Christian church only through the door of Jewry, which was to say that they had to receive the rite of circumcision. That matter was debated at the Jerusalem Council. The Holy Spirit was in control. The pronouncement was made to the gentile churches that it seemed good to the Spirit and the Council to lay upon them no greater burden than certain necessary things, among which circumcision was not numbered. Subsequently, in his letter to the Galatians, Paul violently assailed the Judaistic heresy. He anathematized: 'Though we, or an angel from heaven, preach any other gospel unto you than that which we have preached unto you, let him be accursed' (Gal. 1:8).

Universalism and the Church Today

More than nineteen centuries have elapsed since the Christian church was commissioned and empowered to evangelize the world, and still its work is not done. To the charge of slothfulness the historic church can only plead guilty. But what accounts for this indolence? Many factors have, no doubt, contributed, but the most potent factor has been a deficiency in godliness. The church has not been as God-conscious as it should have been. If the church had always lived in the full consciousness of God's infinite love, God's sovereign election, God's gracious covenant, God's sovereign commission, and of the truth that the God of the Bible is the only true and living God, as well as the God of all the earth, it would have been incomparably more active in the spread of the gospel.

Although much of present-day evangelism is man-centred rather than God-centred, the present age is undeniably the age of missions. From whatever motive, during the nineteenth and twentieth centuries almost all branches of the Christian church have been active as never before in world-wide evangelism. At last the church seems to be fully aware of its God-given task to proclaim the evangel universally.

Is it? Sad to say, even today it cannot truly be asserted that the church has grasped the full meaning of Christian universalism. A few evidences may be cited.

Evangelism among Jews is being neglected. Liberal Protestants feel that to attempt to evangelize a Jew is to insult him and his religion. Judaism and Christianity are esteemed as equally valid, or nearly so. In conferences of Christian and Jewish leaders these religions are placed on a par. On the other hand, there are evangelicals who are convinced that missions to Jews can hardly help proving futile because the curse which they invited by the cry, 'His blood be on us and on our children' (Matt. 27:25), is in effect. Sometimes it is said: 'The Jews have had their chance.' That this reasoning contains a modicum of truth need not be denied. By and large, Israel has hardened its heart. In the words of Paul, 'Blindness is happened to Israel.' But it may not be overlooked that this holds of God's ancient people only 'in part' (Rom. 11:25). By the grace of the Holy Spirit literally thousands of Jews were converted to Christianity at Pentecost. Christ Himself laid hold mightily on a Jew at the gate of Damascus and turned him from a persecutor of Him and His church into the greatest Christian missionary of all time. The conversion of this one Jew has resulted in countless conversions throughout the world and throughout the centuries. Nor may it be forgotten that the Lord Himself designated Saul as His chosen vessel to bear His name, not only 'before the gentiles', but also 'before the children of Israel' (Acts 9: 15). It is meaningful that in his missionary labours Paul customarily brought the gospel 'to the Jew first' (Rom. 1:16). On his arrival in pagan Rome, too, he first of all sought contact with the Jews of that city (Acts 28:17).

In many lands, the United States of America included, there are Caucasian Christians who bar believers of other races, notably Negroes, from membership in the ecclesiastical organization to which they themselves belong. To be sure, they would not withhold the gospel from other races, nor would they deny membership in the spiritual body of Christ to those races. But they do not permit Negroes to participate with them in the same service of worship, nor to celebrate with them the Holy Supper, which was intended by the Lord to signify, among other truths, the unity of believers, as Paul said: 'We being many are one bread and one body: for we are all partakers of that one bread' (I Cor. 10:17). That attitude, although not constituting a denial of Christian universalism, surely betrays a sad lack of understanding of its full implications. Those who take that attitude need to be reminded that in Christ 'there is neither Greek nor Jew, circumcision nor uncircumcision, barbarian, Scythian, bond nor free; but Christ is all, and in all' (Col. 3:11).

Here attention must be called to a much neglected phase of evangelism. When Christian universalism is spoken of, the reference usually is to nations and races. But the concept is not thus exhausted. It applies also to the various strata of society. True though it is that, by and large, Christ's disciples are 'not many wise men after the flesh, not many mighty, not many noble . . . but God hath chosen the foolish things of the world to confound the wise; and God hath chosen the weak things of the world to confound the things that are mighty; and base things of the world, and things which are despised, hath God chosen, yea, and things which are not, to bring to nought things that are: that no flesh should glory in his presence' (I Cor. 1:26–29), yet, in Christ there is neither rich nor poor, educated nor unlearned, ruler nor subject. Generally speaking, churches are wont to concentrate their evangelistic efforts on the destitute and the ignorant, the slum population of the city, those who are said to be 'down' but not yet 'out'. Such surely need the gospel. But bank presidents, corporation heads, government officials, and university professors need it no less. Christ brought the gospel to Nicodemus, a member of the Sanhedrin, the supreme court of the Jews. He saved highly educated and cultured Paul. Philip preached to a man who was over all the treasure of the queen of Ethiopia. In Luke's account of Paul's missionary travels the first recorded convert was Sergius Paulus, governor of Cyprus (Acts 13:4-12). As a result of Paul's labour in the gospel some of Caesar's household became members of the household of faith (Phil. 4:22). Men of high degree need exactly the same evangel as do those of low degree. It is the evangel of a poor sinner and a rich Saviour. All alike must be saved as was the malefactor at the Saviour's right hand on Calvary – by abandoning themselves, as sinners deserving of the divine curse, to the Crucified One.

7: God and the Urgency of Evangelism

NINETEEN CENTURIES HAVE ELAPSED SINCE Christ commissioned His followers to make disciples of all the nations and qualified them by the gift of the Holy Spirit for the performance of that task. Yet, according to the *World Almanac*, Christians throughout the world in the year of our Lord 1960 numbered 869,923,820, the adherents of other religions or none, 1,923,128,180. Those figures, together with the undeniable fact that of those counted as Christians a great many were Christians only in name, point to the extreme urgency of evangelism. However, this chapter will present that theme from another viewpoint – the theological.

Heterodoxy versus Urgent Evangelism

There are theologies which, although they lie far apart from one another, alike obscure, or even deny, the urgency of evangelism.

In one form or another the error of a second probation is rather widely held.

In the opinion of the earliest church fathers, both of the east and the west, and perhaps the greater number of later and modern theologians, the passage I Peter 3:18-20 teaches that in the interval between His death and His resurrection Christ descended into the domain of the dead in order to preach the gospel to Noah's imprisoned contemporaries, who had failed to heed the warnings of that man of God prior to the deluge. Augustine objected to that interpretation and took this passage to mean that it was the Spirit of Christ who preached through Noah to his contemporaries in the days preceding the flood, which persons were in the prison of eternal punishment at the time when Peter wrote this epistle. The latter interpretation became prevalent in the Reformed churches and is advocated by many, although not all, Reformed expositors. If the former construction were to stand, it would not necessarily detract from the urgency of evangelism today, for Christ's descent into hell in order to preach to Noah's contemporaries could be regarded as an isolated instance of a second probation. Nevertheless, that construction would leave room for other possible instances. Thus any doctrine of a trial period after death tends to derogate from the importance of evangelism prior to death.

Throughout the history of Christian doctrine there have been those who argued that, there being no salvation apart from Christ, it would be unjust on the part of God to assign to everlasting perdition such as never heard of Christ during their stay on earth. The conclusion was drawn that those who die in ignorance of the Saviour must somehow after death have an opportunity to receive the gospel of salvation. The truth was overlooked that the entire human race, having sinned in Adam, is deserving of hell. The fact was ignored that the just recompense of any and every sin committed by man is eternal death. Nor was justice done to the statement of Jesus that in the judgment he who knew not and committed things worthy of stripes will be beaten with fewer stripes, to be sure, than he who transgressed wittingly, but will nevertheless be beaten (Luke 12:48). Obviously, the effect of this departure from Scripture can only be to reduce greatly the urgency of evangelism.

Certain cults teach boldly that all who fall short of salvation in this life, also those who have heard the gospel, will have another 'chance at salvation' after death. Jehovah's Witnesses are an outstanding example. If such were true, it would clearly be less urgent for anyone to believe in Christ than it is if everyone who dies in unbelief is irretrievably lost. Just as clearly it would in that case be less than urgent to make the offer of salvation to the unsaved.

Mention must here be made of the denial of the conscious suffering of unbelievers in eternal hell. That denial comes to concrete expression in the teaching of Jehovah's Witnesses that those who fail of salvation on their second probation will be annihilated. The Seventh-day Adventist doctrine of conditional immortality leads to a similar conclusion. Beyond the aforenamed sects, too, the view is widely held that the Scriptural presentation of hell is so completely outdated that he who still accepts it should have been born, to say the least, three hundred years ago, and that it is cause for jesting rather than trembling. But the fact that the infallible Christ has told us in His infallible Word that the wrath of God will abide on those who fail to receive Him in faith (John 3:36), that on the day of judgment He will sentence the unrighteous to everlasting fire, prepared for the devil and his angels (Matt. 25:41, 46), and that the place 'where their worm dieth not and the fire is not quenched' is awful reality (Mark 9:44, 46, 48) makes the preaching of the gospel to the unsaved exceedingly urgent. Conversely, the denial of that fact subtracts greatly from that urgency. And if it be objected that as a matter of fact both Jehovah's Witnesses and the Seventh-day Adventists excel in missionary zeal, the answer lies at hand. They are more concerned about proselytizing than about evangelizing. They are wont to make propaganda, not for the Scriptural gospel of salvation, but rather for their peculiar aberrations from historic Christian truth.

On the theological scene of this day has appeared a mighty resurgence of an error which has confused Christendom ever since the days of Origen, who died about the middle of the third century. It is the heresy of universal salvation. Universalists, Unitarians, and Christian Scientists propound it. Almost all of today's liberals in various denominations subscribe to it. And neo-orthodox Karl Barth, generally rated the most influential theologian of the day, also teaches it, albeit not with complete consistency. It is difficult to conceive of a teaching more inimical to urgent evangelism. If somehow all men are going to share in the eternal bliss of heaven, there is no compelling reason for haste in bringing them the gospel of salvation.

Still another heresy must be named which cannot but detract seriously from the urgency of evangelism. Many avowed Christians are today denying Christianity as the only true religion, Christ as the one and only Saviour, salvation by the grace of God, to the exclusion of human merit, as the sole way of salvation. Christianity is said to be but one of many religions, at the head of the class perhaps, yet in the same class with others. Buddha and Confucius are said to be Saviours, too. And salvation is said to be by character and the practice of such virtues as denial of self and love for neighbours. To say that this view destroys the urgency of evangelism is patently an understatement. The obvious fact is that it leaves no room at all for Christian evangelism.

Orthodoxy and Urgent Evangelism

A note of urgency is unmistakable in Jesus' command,

'The harvest truly is great, but the labourers are few: pray ye therefore the Lord of the harvest, that he would send forth labourers into his harvest' (Luke 10:2).

Throughout the Bible the note of urgency sounds forth pronouncedly in the invitations of the gospel. Following are a few examples.

'Choose you this day whom ye will serve . . . but as for me and my house, we will serve the Lord' (Josh. 24:15).

'How long halt ye between two opinions? If the Lord be God, follow him: but if Baal, then follow him' (I Kings 18:21).

'Today if ye will hear his voice, harden not your heart, as in the provocation, and as in the day of temptation in the wilderness' (Ps. 95:8).

'Ho, every one that thirsteth, come ye to the waters, and he that hath no money; come ye, buy, and eat; yea, come, buy wine and milk without money and without price. Wherefore do ye spend money for that which is not bread? and your labour for that which satisfieth not? Hearken diligently unto me, and eat that which is good, and let your soul delight itself in fatness. Incline your ear, and come unto me: hear, and your soul shall live; and I will make an everlasting covenant with you, even the sure mercies of David' (Isa. 55:1–3).

'As I live, saith the Lord God, I have no pleasure in the death of the wicked; but that the wicked turn from his way and live: turn ye, turn ye from your evil ways; for why will ye die, O house of Israel?' (Ezek. 33:11).

'Come unto me, all ye that labour and are heavy laden, and I will give you rest. Take my yoke upon you, and learn of me; for I am meek and lowly in heart: and ye shall find rest unto your souls. For my yoke is easy, and my burden is light' (Matt. 11:28–30).

'Go into the highways and hedges, and compel them to come in, that my house may be filled' (Luke 14:23).

'Now then, we are ambassadors for Christ, as though God did beseech you by us: we pray you in Christ's stead, be ye reconciled to God' (II Cor. 5:20).

'I have heard thee in a time accepted, and in the day of salvation have I succoured thee: behold, now is the accepted time; behold, now is the day of salvation' (II Cor. 6:2).

'See that ye refuse not him that speaketh. For if they escaped not who refused him that spake on earth, much more shall not we escape, if we turn away from him that speaketh from heaven' (Heb. 12:25).

The reason for the urgency of evangelism lies in God. Because He is who He is, God urgently pleads with sinners to turn to Him.

The God of the Bible is God alone. He is the one living God. All other gods so-called are dumb idols. Therefore it behoves men to turn from every form of idolatry to Him, and to do so abruptly, summarily.

Only the God of the Bible is able to save. Salvation belongs to the Triune God. No one can come in faith to the Son except the Father draw him (John 6:44). The Son is the way, the truth, the life; no man can come to the Father but by Him (John 14:6). And none can own Jesus as Lord but by the Holy Spirit (I Cor. 12:3). That being true, it behoves the sinner to flee, helpless, to God for salvation, and to do so without delay.

The God of the Bible is altogether just and righteous. 'Righteousness and judgment are the habitation of his throne' (Ps. 97:2). Never does He depart so much as a hair-breadth from the path of perfect justice. If He did, He would be denying Himself, which is the one thing God cannot do (II Tim. 2:13). He who takes the statement, 'Mercy rejoiceth against judgment' (James 2:14), to mean that the divine mercy renders the divine justice inoperative is guilty of the most careless sort of exegesis. The reference is to nothing of the kind. Having said that he who has shown no mercy will be judged by God without mercy, James adds that contrariwise he who has led a life of Christian mercy may approach the judgment seat of God without fear and even with joy. In short, the meaning is that there is no condemnation for him who has true faith; that is to say, 'faith which worketh by love' (Gal. 5:6). From the beginning the justice of God decreed that the penalty of sin would be death (Gen. 2:17). That 'the wages of sin is death' (Rom. 6:23), is a law as unalterable as is God Himself. And death involves alienation from God, even everlasting separation from Him. Such a God confronts the sinner. Well may he, driven as by tempest, run to Calvary, kneel as a hell-deserving sinner at the foot of the cross, and eagerly, ardently, passionately, accept reconciliation with God through the atoning blood of Him who hangs on the accursed tree.

The God of the Bible is love (I John 4:8, 16), even infinite love. To infer, as many do, that He cannot possibly condemn any creature of His to eternal suffering in hell is not only to contradict the Son of God, who is love incarnate, but also to ignore the obvious truth that precisely because the love of God is infinite those who fail to requite that love are deserving of lowest hell. God's love being infinite, it is a sin of infinite proportions to spurn that love. Yet that is done by those who reject God's Son, the gift of His love, by unbelief. God has manifested His infinite love by sending His only begotten Son into the world in order that He might die for the ungodly (Rom. 5:6). And in infinite love He assures sinners everywhere that He 'will have all men to be saved' (I Tim. 2:4) and is 'not willing that any should perish, but that all should come to repentance' (II Peter 3:9). To reject such love is to incur everlasting banishment from the presence of God. To respond to it in faith and love is to inherit life everlasting. Nothing can be more urgent than the choice between these.

Christ's Return and Urgent Evangelism

In reply to the query of His disciples what would be the sign of His coming and of the end of the world, Jesus predicted deception by false prophets, wars and rumours of wars, famines, pestilences, and earthquakes, persecution of His followers, abounding iniquity. He added expressly that the end would not come until the gospel of the kingdom had been preached in all the world for a witness unto all nations (Matt 24:3-14). The latter statement is not surprising. God has His elect in every nation, and all of the elect must be gathered in before the day of final judgment. Also, on that day no nation will be able to plead ignorance of the gospel.

The fact that Christ will not return so long as the gospel has not been preached to all nations has a direct and strong bearing on the urgency of evangelism.

Beyond all doubt, the day of Christ's second coming is fully determined in the eternal plan of God. God knows that day, not only because He is omniscient (Matt. 24:36) but because He Himself has fixed it in His counsel of foreordination. But also included in that counsel are all the events that are antecedent and prerequisite to Christ's return. Prominent among those events is the proclamation of the gospel to all nations. The same divine decree that determines the day of Jesus' coming demands world-wide evangelism prior to that day.

It may be said without hesitation that Christ cannot return unless the gospel is first brought to all nations. When the ship on which Paul was being brought to Italy was caught in a violent storm, God assured him that not a life would be lost, and Paul communicated that assurance to the sailors and soldiers aboard. But when, a short time later, the sailors attempted to rescue themselves by taking to the lifeboat, Paul said: 'Except these abide in the ship, ye cannot be saved' (Acts 27:23–31). The point of the illustration is that, while God's counsel is sure to stand, in its execution He employs responsible men.

The conclusion is fully warranted that evangelism contributes to Christ's return. The assertion is wholly in order, that by the preaching of the gospel the church makes an *indispensable* contribution to His coming.

For Christ's early return the church longs and prays. To His announcement, 'Surely I come quickly', it replies: 'Even so, come, Lord Jesus' (Rev. 22:20). And by evangelizing the world it *works* for His early return.

Why is it that the church longs and prays and works for the Lord's early return? Is it because that event will mark the complete salvation of the saints, the wresting of their bodies from the power of death, and the receiving of their incorruptible bodies, united with their perfect souls, into the glory of heaven? No doubt! Is it because that event will spell the ultimate triumph of the saints over all their enemies? Beyond question!

But there are higher considerations. The Saviour's return will bring glory, not merely to the saints, but to God and His Christ. It will mean the perfection of Christ's body, the church; the vindication of the Christ, who then will judge and justly condemn the world, which once sat in judgment on Him and unjustly sentenced Him to death; the universal recognition of Christ as King and the glorification of God by the whole of creation, for at the name of Jesus every knee will bow, of things in heaven, and things in earth, and things under the earth, and every tongue will confess that Jesus Christ is Lord, to the glory of God the Father (Phil. 2:10, 11), and, all things having been subjected to the Son, He will 'also himself be subject unto him that put all things under him, that God may be all in all' (I Cor. 15:28).

What, above all else, makes Christian evangelism urgent is its contribution to the hastening of the day when God shall receive all the glory due to His great and holy name.

8: God and the Motive of Evangelism

IN THE COURSE OF ITS HISTORY THE CHRISTIAN church has been actuated by various motives in the spread of the gospel. Many of these motives were noble, but others – it must be admitted – were ignoble. For example, there is reason to think that in the heyday of colonialism missions were sometimes employed to the end of gaining dominion over primitive peoples and extracting wealth from their resources. Under the flag of a so-called Christian nation soldiers and prospectors would accompany the missionary, and in some instances there seems to have been more concern about the flag than about the banner of the cross. Quite apart from the question whether or not colonialism is to be condemned as an unmitigated evil, such use of the evangel as a means to a mundane and material end can only be adjudged an insult to both the gospel of Christ and the Christ of the gospel.

However, the purpose of this study is not so much to assess the motives that have in the course of history operated in evangelistic effort as to discover the demands of Scripture for the motivation of evangelism.

Love of Self as a Motive of Evangelism

As was pointed out previously, self-love is not in itself evil. Rather, it is a good. Man loves himself because he bears the image of God, who loves Himself. God bestowed divine approbation on self-love when He commanded man to love his neighbour as himself (Matt. 19:19) and when

He enjoined husbands to love their wives as their own bodies (Eph. 5:28). Yet, fallen man being what he is, love of self is easily perverted into selfishness. And selfishness not only is sin but lies at the root of all sin.

The Pharisees of Jesus' day were motivated by selfish pride and hypocritical legalism when they compassed sea and land to make one proselyte and, having made one, rendered him twice the child of hell that they themselves were (Matt. 23:15). On the Judaizers in the apostolic church Paul passed the judgment: 'As many as desire to make a fair show in the flesh, they constrain you to be circumcised; only lest they should suffer persecution for the cross of Christ. For neither they themselves who are circumcised keep the law; but desire to have you circumcised that they may glory in your flesh' (Gal. 6:12, 13). Instead of seeking the spiritual good of gentile converts to Christianity, the Judaizers were on the lookout for their own comfort and glory. They insisted on circumcision for those converts in order that they themselves might escape the opprobrium of the cross and, instead, might gain glory for their strictness in the externals of religion.

We of today need to be on our guard against selfish motivation in evangelism. The minister who would become a missionary to a backward people in order to escape the onerous task of preaching to an educated audience in the homeland is guilty of selfishness. So is the man or the woman who would bring the gospel to a distant land because of the halo which in the estimation of sentimental folk is wont to surround foreign missionaries. So is he or she who, troubled by an inferiority complex in civilized America, reckons that a sense of superiority over uncivilized Africans is a thing to be grasped. So is the missionary who places adventure above, or on a par with, evangelization. And the same is true of the person who engages in evangelism in order to make a display of personal piety.

On the other hand, there is a legitimate, and even laudable self-love which may properly play a part in the motivation of evangelism. If one feels an inner compulsion to evangelism, a compulsion which leaves him no rest unless and until he yields to it, he may well in the interest of peace of mind devote his life to evangelistic labours. Paul was no stranger to such a sense of compulsion. Of it he said: 'Though I preach the gospel, I have nothing to glory of: for necessity is laid upon me; yea, woe is unto me, if I preach not the gospel. For if I do this thing willingly, I have a reward: but if against my will, a dispensation of the gospel is committed unto me' (I Cor. 9: 16, 17). It may not be inferred that Paul preached the gospel unwillingly. Beyond all doubt, he did it gladly and with loving devotion. Repeatedly he called himself 'a slave of Jesus Christ' (Rom. 1:1 RSV, footnote), but it was his heart's most fervent desire to be precisely that. And so it may be added that, if one has a desire to bring the gospel to the unsaved, a desire which is not weak but compelling, not ephemeral but persistent in spite of seemingly insuperable obstacles and an irrepressible sense of one's unworthiness of, and insufficiency for, so glorious and so exacting a task, it is perfectly proper for him in the interest of his own satisfaction and happiness to yield to that desire.

At this point, however, a reservation of the greatest importance must be made. He who yields to such compulsion and to such a desire may indeed do so for his own sake. Yet, that is by no means the whole truth. It is but one aspect, and not at all the most weighty, of the situation. He should yield also for the sake of those to whom he would bring the gospel. And, most important of all, he should yield for the sake of God, the author of that compulsion and that desire. Because they are of God, they must also be unto Him. In the words of that devout and diligent student of the New Testament, Johann Albrecht Bengel: 'He who loves God will love himself in a proper degree, without selfishness.' That is a way of saying, not only that his love for God will keep him from the sin of selfishness, but also that his love for self flows forth from his love for God.

Love of Neighbours as a Motive of Evangelism

When He was asked which is the great commandment in the law, the Lord Jesus replied: 'Thou shalt love the Lord thy God with all thy heart, and with all thy soul, and with all thy mind. This is the first and great commandment.' And in the same breath he added: 'And the second is like unto it, Thou shalt love thy neighbour as thyself' (Matt. 22:37–39). He could hardly have stressed the necessity of love for neighbours more than by equating God's demand for it with the divine demand of love for God.

In the parable of the good Samaritan (Luke 10:29–39) Jesus has taught us that all men are our neighbours, those included whom we deem farthest removed from us, not merely geographically, but also culturally, and even religiously.

It follows unavoidably that the Christian, in bringing the gospel to the unsaved, must be motivated by love for them. This motive is not only desirable, however highly, but necessary. Paul gave well-nigh unbelievably strong expression to the love which actuated him in preaching Christ to the Jews of his day when he testified with a solemn oath: 'I say the truth in Christ, I lie not, my conscience also bearing me witness in the Holy Ghost, that I have great heaviness and continual sorrow in my heart. For I could wish that myself were accursed from Christ for my brethren, my kinsmen according to the flesh' (Rom. 9:1-3).

A significant distinction must here be made. The Bible speaks of two sorts of love for neighbours. On the one hand, it recognizes that unregenerate man is capable of loving his fellows and often does so. Said Jesus: 'If ye love them which love you, what thank have ye? for sinners also love those that love them' (Luke 6:32). But His disciples He enjoined: 'Love your enemies, do good to them which hate you' (Luke 6:27). The former love is restricted to friends; the latter extends to enemies. The former is a product of the common grace of God; the latter is a fruit of saving grace. The former dwells in him who is devoid of love for God and even hates God; the latter issues from love for God. It is that love for neighbours which God requires in His law. The two tables of the law, the first demanding love for God, the second love for neighbours, are inseparable. The second is based upon, rather rooted in, the first. We should love our neighbours because we love God. Only when we do that, do we love them as God would have us. The preamble of the decalogue, 'I am the Lord thy God, which have brought thee out of the land of Egypt, out of the house of bondage' (Exod. 20:2), introduces the second table as well as the first. In gratitude to God for His salvation we must love both God and our fellows. God's law requires that we love God for His own sake; it also demands that we love our fellows for God's sake.

Which love for neighbours must motivate him who

[99]

would bring the evangel to the unsaved is not difficult to say. That love which is the product of common grace alone is quite insufficient, for it will seek the temporal and material good of men, but hardly their spiritual and eternal welfare. That love which is restricted to friends is utterly inadequate, for the bearer of the gospel must love those who persecute him and pray for them, as did the Lord Jesus when He pleaded for those who were nailing Him to the cross: 'Father, forgive them; for they know not what they do' (Luke 23:34), and as Stephen did when he interceded for those who were stoning him to death: 'Lord, lay not this sin to their charge' (Acts 7:60). And, obviously, that love for man which is divorced from love for God and co-exists with hatred of God cannot possibly serve as a motive for proclaiming the gospel of the grace of God. Only he who has been born of the Spirit of God, who loves his neighbours because he loves God, who loves his enemies, blesses them that curse him, does good to them that hate him, prays for them which despitefully use him and persecute him, and thus manifests himself to be a child of the heavenly Father (Matt. 5:44, 45), has the proper motive for offering the Christ of the gospel to sinful men.

Love of God the Motive of Evangelism

The sum of what was said about love of self and love of neighbours as motives of evangelism is that they are proper motives only if they spring from love of God. The ultimate motive of evangelism, then, must be love of God. It is *the* motive of evangelism, embracing and excelling all other worthy motives.

Here let it be recorded that human love, that of the

Christian, too, is dependent on something lovely in its object. Often that makes it difficult for the Christian to love his neighbour. Some men are so depraved that it is next to impossible to love them. Not infrequently the Christian finds it difficult to love himself. Because of his sins and his sinfulness he abhors himself. But the believer has no such difficulty with God in Christ. He is 'the rose of Sharon', 'the lily of the valleys' (Song of Solomon 2:1), 'the chiefest among ten thousand' (Song of Solomon 5:10), the 'altogether lovely' (Song of Solomon 5:16). God Himself is love itself, for 'God is love' (I John 4:8, 16).

By denying the Master, Peter had forfeited his apostleship. But in boundless grace the risen Lord had in mind to restore him to that exalted office. Before that could be done, Peter had to make a confession. It was a confession of love. Thrice he had affirmed in the palace of the high priest that he did not know the Nazarene. Violently he had vowed that he did not love him. Now, at the Sea of Tiberias, thrice the question was put to him: 'Simon, son of Jonas, lovest thou me?' It was a humiliating question. No longer was he Peter, the rock, the apostle. Once more he was what he had been before he was called by Jesus, just Simon, son of Jonas. It was a question that cut to the quick. His love for his Saviour was being called into question, and rightly so. Well might his answers excel in self-effacement. The Lord's query was, 'Lovest thou me more than these?' No doubt, the reference was to Peter's boast, 'Although all shall be offended, yet will not I' (Mark 14:29). In his reply Peter evaded the phrase 'more than these', and for the Saviour's word for *love* he substituted another. According to that competent commentator, F. L. Godet, he said in substance: 'Thou inquirest whether I love Thee in the highest spiritual sense of the term; I can only say that I love Thee with a love of personal attachment.' Only in His third query did Jesus condescend to use Peter's word for *love*. In effect He asked: 'Dost thou truly love Me with an emotional love?' And Peter, acknowledging that to all appearances his behaviour belied his protestation of even that love, appealed to the divine omniscience as proof of it. For the present purpose the significant fact is that only after the Saviour had received the assurance of Peter's love did He charge him: 'Feed my lambs', 'Tend my sheep' (ASV), and 'Feed my sheep' (John 21: 15-17). That charge was conditioned on Peter's love for Christ. The inference is fully warranted that he who would bring the gospel to Christ's sheep of whatever fold, also to those of His sheep which have not yet been brought into the fold, must needs be motivated by love for Christ.

There is a passage of Scripture which teaches the same lesson emphatically but is often misunderstood. The reference is to Paul's words in II Corinthians 5: 14, 'The love of Christ constraineth us.' The love of Christ here spoken of is not the love of Christ's disciples for Him but the love of Christ for His disciples; and *to constrain* does not mean *to drive onward* but, contrariwise, *to confine, to inhibit*. As the following verse clearly indicates, the apostle says that the love for His own, which Christ manifested in dying for them, should control them in such a way that henceforth they live, not unto themselves, but unto Him. However, that statement does have implications for the love of believers for their Saviour. They love Him because He first loved them (I John 4: 19). And it is their love for Him which indeed keeps them from living unto themselves but also compels them to devote their lives to Him. Commenting on this passage, Calvin said beautifully: 'The knowledge of the measureless love of Christ, of which He furnished us with an evidence in His death, ought to constrain our affections, that they may go in no other direction than that of loving Him in return. . . . Every one that truly ponders that wonderful love becomes, as it were, bound to Him, and constrained by the closest tie; and devotes himself wholly to His service.' No aspect of His service is more important than the spread of His gospel.

Love for God and His Christ guarantees on the part of the believer loving, hence genuine and devoted, in distinction from external and legalistic, obedience to the divine command to evangelize the nations.

Love for God and His Christ will cause the bearer of the evangel to persist in the face of bitter disappointment. At times, even over extended periods, it may seem to him that the seed of the gospel sown by him has fallen only by the wayside or in stony places or among thorns, and that none of it has sprouted in good ground (Matt. 13:3–8); but his motto will remain *Nil desperandum, Deo duce*. With God as his leader, he will never despair. His love for God, inseparable as it is from his faith in God, will keep him from falling into the slough of despondency.

Love for God and His Christ will enable the Christian to witness boldly for Christ in the face of persecution. Repeatedly it is said in the Acts of the Apostles that the early disciples did just that (Acts 4:13, 29, 31). The Bible teaches that every true disciple of Christ is bound to suffer persecution at the hands of the world. Said Jesus: 'Remember the word that I said unto you, The servant is not greater than his lord. If they have persecuted me, they will also persecute you' (John 15:20). Paul informed recent converts in Asia Minor: 'We must through much tribulation enter into the kingdom' (Acts 14:22). Jesus' eight beatitudes are not descriptions of so many kinds of Christians, but statements of so many marks of every Christian. The last one reads: 'Blessed are they which are persecuted for righteousness' sake: for theirs is the kingdom of heaven. Blessed are ye, when men shall revile you, and persecute you, and shall say all manner of evil against you falsely, for my sake. Rejoice, and be exceeding glad; for great is your reward in heaven: for so persecuted they the prophets that were before you' (Matt. 5:10–12). The concluding words of that beatitude inform us that of the persecution which is common to believers those who prophesied in the name of the Lord have in history had to bear the brunt. The same truth was expressed by Jesus when, in pronouncing His woes on the holy city, he addressed it as 'Jerusalem, that killest the prophets and stonest them which are sent unto thee' (Matt. 23:37). And James, brother of Jesus, encouraged his readers: 'Take, my brethren, the prophets, who have spoken in the name of the Lord, for an example of suffering affliction, and of patience' (James 5:10). Persecution, then, is not incidental to prophesying but an ordained element of the prophet's life. And he who witnesses for Christ and His evangel is a prophet. If he truly loves Christ, as he must, persecution will not deter him from witnessing. Contrariwise, he will walk in the footsteps of those apostles who, when they had been scourged by the Jewish Sanhedrin for speaking in the name of Jesus, 'departed from the presence of the council, rejoicing that they were counted worthy to suffer shame for his name' (Acts 5:41). One of those apostles was Peter. He both practised what he preached and preached what he practised, for later on he penned the exhortation: 'If any man suffer as a Christian, let him not be ashamed; but let him glorify God on this behalf' (I Peter 4:16).

Love for God and His Christ will induce, yes compel, God's child to devote himself wholeheartedly to the spread of the evangel because he knows that its ultimate end will be the glorification of God and Christ. Through evangelism the day will be hastened when 'every tongue shall confess that Jesus Christ is Lord, to the glory of God the Father' (Phil. 2:11). That is the chiefest concern of him who loves God.

9: God and the Aim of Evangelism

TO MANY THE QUESTION AS TO WHAT IS THE AIM
of evangelism presents no problem whatever. They think
it a foregone conclusion that its one and only aim is the
salvation of souls. In fact, however, the matter is not
nearly so simple. The conversion of sinners is indeed an
aim of evangelism, and an important one, but it has additional aims. And its highest and ultimate end is not the
welfare of men, not even their eternal bliss, but the glorification of God.

The Salvation of Souls

Man is immortal. He has an eternal destiny. But that
destiny is not the same for all. Some will inherit everlasting
life; others will suffer everlasting death. Some will enjoy
never-ending communion with God; others will be banished from God's presence for ever.

Which of these it will be for a given individual depends
on whether or not he believes on Him whose name is the
only name given under heaven by which men must be
saved (Acts 4 : 12).

That being the case, it is a matter of supreme moment
that all men everywhere become acquainted with that
name. And to bring that about is the task of evangelism.

Well may the evangelist have a passion for souls! In
fact, it is strange beyond comprehension that there are
those who, professing to subscribe to the truth that only
those who believe in Christ will be saved and that all others

[106]

are bound for eternal hell, yet in no way exert themselves to persuade men to depart from the road that leads to destruction and to walk the road to heaven. One cannot help wondering whether these really believe what they say. The issue truly is one of eternal weal or eternal woe.

Paul the missionary had a passion for souls. 'Knowing the terror of the Lord' (II Cor. 5:11), he laboured to persuade men to faith in Christ. He besought, prayed, verily begged, men to be reconciled to God (II Cor. 5:20). He went to great lengths of self-denial in order that he might win others to Christ. Said he: 'Though I be free from all men, yet have I made myself servant unto all, that I might gain the more. And unto the Jews I became as a Jew, that I might gain the Jews; to them that are under the law, as under the law, that I might gain them that are under the law; to them that are without law, as without law (being not without law to God, but under the law to Christ) that I might gain them that are without law. To the weak became I as weak, that I might gain the weak. I am made all things to all men, that I might by all means save some' (I Cor. 9:19-22). While engaged in evangelistic labours in the heathen city of Ephesus, that stronghold of the great Diana, for three whole years he 'ceased not to warn every one night and day with tears' (Acts 20:31). Unbelievable though it may seem, he wished that he himself might be accursed from Christ if only the Jewish nation, his kinsmen after the flesh, might turn to Christ (Rom. 9:3).

Who will care to deny that the Lord Jesus had a passion for souls? On more than one occasion during His public ministry He was 'moved with compassion' toward the multitudes that followed Him 'because they were as sheep not having a shepherd' (Mark 6:34). Tenderly He called: 'Come unto me, all ye that labour and are heavy laden, and I will give you rest. Take my yoke upon you, and learn of me; for I am meek and lowly in heart; and ye shall find rest unto your souls. For my yoke is easy, and my burden is light' (Matt. 11:28-30). From a heart running over with pity He wailed: 'O Jerusalem, Jerusalem . . . how often would I have gathered thy children together, even as a hen gathereth her chickens under her wings, and ye would not!' (Matt. 23:37). He came 'to seek and to save that which was lost' (Luke 19:10), derelicts like Zacchaeus, the publican. When the Pharisees and scribes objected to His receiving sinners and eating with them, He justified His behaviour by telling the surpassingly simple and inimitably affectionate parables of the lost sheep, the lost coin, and the lost son, all three alike conveying the beautiful lesson that there is joy in heaven because of the conversion of a sinner, be it but one (Luke 15). He described Himself as the good shepherd who loves His sheep so inestimably as to give His life for them (John 10:11). So great was 'the breadth and length and depth and height' (Eph. 3:18, 19) of His love that He died for the ungodly (Rom. 5:6). And this means, not merely that He consented in their behalf to the temporary separation of His body and His soul, but that He was willingly forsaken of God in the stead of hell-deserving sinners.

If one may employ an anthropopathism and ascribe human feelings to God, God has a passion for souls. The so-called parable of the lost or prodigal son is more accurately denominated the parable of the loving father. The father, not the son, is the chief *persona dramatis*. Not the son's waywardness, nor even his repentance, is the theme, but the father's love for his perverse child. Ever since the son's departure into a far country, the father's heart had yearned for him. When the returning penitent 'was yet a great way off, his father saw him, and had compassion, and ran, and fell on his neck, and kissed him'. The best robe was put on him; a ring, as evidence of sonship, was placed on his hand, and shoes on his feet. The fatted calf was prepared for dinner; there was feasting and great merriment. The father jubilated: 'This my son was dead and is alive again; he was lost and is found' (Luke 15: 11–24). Such is the love of God for sinners. He assures the erring: 'Have I any pleasure at all that the wicked should die, and not that he should return from his ways and live?' (Ezek. 18: 23). 'For God so loved the world, that he gave his only begotten Son, that whosoever believeth in him should not perish, but have everlasting life' (John 3: 16).

The Growth of Christ's Church

By and large, the church is not highly regarded today. Those on the outside think of it at best as a mildly beneficent, although not overly useful, institution. Even many evangelicals, themselves church members, regard it as a temporary and inferior substitute for the kingdom which Christ meant to establish at His first coming but, when the Jewish people rejected Him as king, postponed until His second advent. Because the church is not esteemed as it should be, its growth is not wont to be stressed as an aim of evangelism.

Now that is not as it ought to be, for the Bible puts much stress on the truth that all who receive Christ in faith by that very act become members of Christ's body, the church.

In the Great Commission Christ commanded His followers, not only to make disciples of all the nations, but also to baptize them (Matt. 28: 19). Therefore from the very outset it was customary in the apostolic church to baptize converts to Christianity. Approximately three thousand were converted on the day of Pentecost, and all of these were at once baptized (Acts 2:41). As soon as the Ethiopian eunuch confessed his faith in Christ, he was baptized. No time was lost. The evangelist Philip baptized him in a pool of water by the roadside (Acts 8:36-38). Ananias of Damascus baptized Saul of Tarsus immediately upon his conversion (Acts 9:18). When Cornelius, the centurion, and those in his house believed, Peter ordered them to be baptized (Acts 10:47, 48). Paul and Silas baptized the believing Philippian jailer and his household in the very night of their conversion (Acts 16:33). Other instances could be cited. Now baptism signified, among other blessings, reception into the Christian church, wherefore Paul told the believers of his day that they were 'all baptized into one body' (I Cor. 12:13). Beyond all doubt, he referred to the body of Christ, the church.

From another statement made by Paul to the Corinthian church it has sometimes been inferred that baptism, and hence membership in the visible church, is relatively inconsequential. Said the apostle: 'Christ sent me not to baptize, but to preach the gospel' (I Cor. 1:17). But the inference is manifestly erroneous. It is quite inconceivable that Paul would brush aside lightly Christ's emphatic command to baptize such as become His disciples. Rather, in the consciousness that the chief design of his apostolic mission was teaching, Paul recognized that baptizing could well be left to his associates. It is worthy of note that Peter, too, instead of himself baptizing Cornelius and his fellow converts, had others perform that rite. Significantly, he *commanded* that they be baptized (Acts 10:48). In view of the multitude of converts, such was for the apostolic age a salutary division of duties. And so the fact remains that in the early church converts were invariably and, on their profession of faith, forthwith received by baptism into the fellowship of believers.

Acts 2 : 47 presents a most significant teaching. It reads : 'The Lord added to the church daily such as should be saved.' The Lord here spoken of is, no doubt, the Lord Jesus Christ, the Head of the church. By His Spirit He wrought saving faith in the hearts of sinners, and He did that daily. But that was not all. All who were thus saved He 'added to the church'. The Head of the church not only required of them to unite with the church, He Himself joined them to the church. Clearly, Christ Himself would have His church grow through evangelism.

It follows that the Roman Catholic Church errs in teaching that membership in the church is prerequisite to salvation. The truth of the matter is that church membership is a normal and necessary consequence of salvation. But it also follows that those Protestant evangelists are in serious error who belittle church membership by driving a wedge between Christianity and what they disparagingly call 'churchianity'.

What, more than aught else, makes the growth of the church meaningful is the fact that it enhances the glory of Christ Jesus, the church's Head and King. As the author of Proverbs put it, 'In the multitude of people is the king's honour' (Prov. 14 : 28). And the seer on the isle of Patmos had in mind principally the glory of Christ and God when he recorded this vision of the church triumphant : 'Lo, a great multitude, which no man could number, of all nations, and kindreds, and peoples, and tongues, stood before the throne, and before the Lamb, clothed with white robes, and palms in their hands; and cried with a loud voice, saying, Salvation to our God which sitteth upon the throne, and unto the Lamb' (Rev. 7:9, 10).

The Coming of Christ's Kingdom

Significantly, the gospel which Jesus preached is described as 'the gospel of the kingdom' (Matt. 4:23). It is no less significant that, when, on returning from his third missionary journey, the apostle Paul bade farewell to the elders of the Ephesian church, he reminded them that he had preached among them 'the kingdom of God' and identified that message with 'the gospel of the grace of God' (Acts 20:24, 25).

The term *kingdom of Christ* has come to be used in more senses than one. Theologians distinguish between the kingdom of His grace and the kingdom of His power. The former is identical with the church. Paul had it in mind when he exhorted the believers at Colosse to give thanks to the Father, 'who', said he, 'hath delivered us from the power of darkness, and hath translated us into the kingdom of his dear Son' (Col. 1:13). *The Westminster Confession of Faith* defines the visible church as 'the kingdom of the Lord Jesus Christ' (XXV, 2). The kingdom of Christ's power extends over all things, the whole of the universe. 'All power', said he, 'is given unto me in heaven and in earth' (Matt. 28:18). The kingdom in this sense is named in Answer 191 of *The Westminster Larger Catechism*. Besides, theologians often speak of the kingdom of Christ's glory, by which they mean the ultimate universal recognition of Christ as King in the day when all His enemies shall have been put under His feet (I Cor. 15:25). Commenting on the second petition of the Lord's Prayer, *The Westminster Shorter Catechism* says: 'We pray . . .

[112]

that the kingdom of grace may be advanced . . . and that the kingdom of glory may be hastened' (Answer 102).

Evangelism has to do with all three of the aforenamed aspects of Christ's kingdom. A significant aim of evangelism is the extension of the kingdom of Christ's grace by the conversion of sinners and their addition to the church. Because Christ has all authority and power on earth and in heaven He has sovereignly commissioned His church to make disciples of all the nations, teaching them to observe His commandments; He enables the church to accomplish that task; and He overrules the doings of His foes unto the coming of His kingdom. Inasmuch as Christ will not return until the gospel of the kingdom has been preached in all the world for a witness unto all nations (Matt. 24:14), evangelism may be said to hasten the day of the consummation of Christ's kingdom of glory.

The aforesaid matters have received consideration either in this chapter or in earlier ones and will on occasion be dealt with again. What needs to be stressed at this juncture is a much neglected phase of the aim of evangelism. It is to persuade men to acknowledge Christ as King over every sphere of human activity, over the entire domain of human life.

Ours is an age of secularism. Life is wont to be divided into two compartments, each of which is hermetically sealed from the other: the religious and the secular. Everyday life is divorced from God. Religion is at most a matter of church attendance, the family altar, and private devotions, but not of business, politics, or education. This sin is rampant in so-called Christian lands. The interpretation of the separation of church and state as the separation of religion and politics is a most serious American fallacy. The banishment of religion from public school education is rapidly destroying the spiritual and moral fibre of the American people. The slogan that business is business, implying that it is not religion, underlies prevalent deception and corruption.

What is secularism but the denial of the Scriptural teaching that Christ is 'the head over all things' (Eph. 1 : 22)?

What the self-styled Christian nations must learn and what the Christian Church must teach the nations of the world is that Christ is King as well as Saviour, and that His kingship extends, not only over the church, but over society in all of its ramifications; for a few examples, over politics, both national and international, over industry and labour, over science and education, over literature and art. That is unmistakably explicit in Christ's charge to His church, 'Teaching them to observe all things whatsoever I have commanded you' (Matt. 28 : 20).

Much is being said and written about totalitarianism. Two types of totalitarianism are vying with each other for supremacy. On the one hand is the totalitarian state. It comes to bold expression in Communist Russia and China and asserts itself somewhat more subtly in a worldwide trend toward statism. The danger that the United Nations will develop into a super-state is anything but imaginary. On the other hand is the totalitarian church. It is represented, not only by the Romish Church, but also by the modernist Protestant ecumenical movement. That the World Council of Churches, gravely contaminated with theological liberalism, will grow into a super-church is by no means impossible and is even probable. Neither of these brands of totalitarianism is much better than the other. Both are immense evils. And woe to humanity if the two ever make common cause! Yet, according to Revelation 13, that is precisely what will come to pass in the days of the Antichrist. Both politically and religiously the human race, with the exception of those whose names are written in the Lamb's book of life, will be consolidated under his rule. But there is a God-appointed totalitarian Ruler. He is 'Head of the church' (Col. 1:18) as well as 'Lord of lords and King of kings' (Rev. 17:14). He has authority over all men and nations and over the entire life of all men and nations. His name is the Christ of God.

The universal recognition of his totalitarian kingship is an essential aim of evangelism.

> Let every kindred, every tribe,
>   On this terrestrial ball,
> To Him all majesty ascribe,
>   And crown Him Lord of all.

Let it not be forgotten that only those who have received Christ as Saviour will honour Him as Lord and King. His kingship presupposes His crucifixion. His kingdom is founded on Calvary. Here, too, the saying applies, 'No cross, no crown'. Those who proclaim Christ as King but deny the atonement wrought by His shed blood are but beating the air. Christ's kingdom divorced from His vicarious death is a castle that exists only in man's imagination.

On the other hand, he who believes in Christ as his Saviour is bound to honour Him as his King. He who truly believes in Him cannot do otherwise. He will glory in both Christ's cross and Christ's crown.

The Glory of God

Every believing student of Scripture will grant that the ultimate end of all things is the glorification of God. Nothing could be clearer than that. 'For of him, and through him, and to him, are all things: to whom be glory for ever. Amen' (Rom. 11:36).

The salvation of souls, the growth of Christ's church, even the coming of Christ's kingdom, of momentous importance though they may be and actually are, are but means to a still higher end, the highest of all ends – God's glorification.

Several passages of Scripture teach that explicitly and emphatically. The following are some of them.

Outstanding in Christ's high-priestly prayer is a note of evangelism. For instance, referring to His disciples, the Saviour said: 'As thou hast sent me into the world, even so have I also sent them into the world' (John 17:18). At least as prominent is the theme of the glorification of Christ and God. It is named not fewer than eight times. For example, Christ prayed: 'Father, I will that they also, whom thou hast given me, be with me where I am, that they may behold the glory which thou hast given me' (John 17:24); and He testified: 'Father, I have glorified thee on the earth: I have finished the work which thou gavest me to do' (John 17:4). It is evident that the Saviour regarded the salvation of men as a means to the end of the glorification of God.

In the conclusion of his letter to the church at Rome Paul related to each other in the most direct way the preaching of the gospel in the gentile world and the glory of God. He wrote: 'Now to him that is of power to stablish you according to my gospel, and the preaching of Jesus Christ, according to the revelation of the mystery, which was kept secret since the world began, but now is made manifest, and by the Scriptures of the prophets, according to the commandment of the everlasting God, made known to all nations for the obedience of faith: to God only wise, be glory through Jesus Christ for ever. Amen' (Rom. 16: 25–27).

Speaking of Christ's exaltation, the same inspired apostle asserted that the universal recognition of His lordship will be 'to the glory of God the Father' (Phil. 2: 11).

'When all things shall be subdued unto him, then shall the Son also himself be subject unto him that put all things under him, that God may be all in all' (I Cor. 15: 28).

10: God and the Agent of Evangelism

BEYOND DISPUTE, THE CHRISTIAN CHURCH IS the God-appointed agent of evangelism. However, when making that statement one does well to define the term *church*. In this context it has two references, which, although inseparable, are properly distinguished from each other. Both the church as an organization, operating through its special offices, and the church as an organism of believers, each of which holds a general or universal office, are God-ordained agents of evangelism.

What follows is a Scriptural substantiation, together with an elaboration, of that twofold proposition.

The Church as an Organization

Not all churches have the same degree of organization. Some are wont to ordain officers; others have no such practice. Nor do all churches that have officers recognize the same number of offices. Yet, unavoidably every church has a measure of organization. And Scripture requires that. It was the invariable custom of the missionary Paul to organize groups of believers as churches. In Asia Minor he and Barnabas ordained elders in every church (Acts 14:23).

The Bible teaches plainly that evangelism is a task of the organized church.

The apostles, to whom the church's Head gave the missionary command, were the foundation of the New Testament organized church. When Peter, as spokesman of the twelve, had confessed Jesus to be the Christ, the Son of the living God, the Lord said: 'I say unto thee that thou art Peter, and upon this rock I will build my church' (Matt. 16:18). The 'rock' of which He spoke was neither Peter as an individual nor merely his confession, but the confessing Peter as representative of the apostles. And the 'church' of which He spoke was an organization, as appears from the fact that He went on to assign to the apostles 'the keys of the kingdom of heaven' (Matt. 16:19; 18:18), thus authorizing them to lay down the conditions for membership in His church. It is evident that both historically and doctrinally the apostles were the foundation of the organized New Testament church. To change the metaphor, the apostles were that church in embryo. It follows that, when Christ charged His apostles to make disciples of all the nations, He gave that command to them and to the organized church of succeeding times.

Pentecost is not the birthday of the Christian church. The church came into being in the garden of Eden. Yet, some truly great changes came over the church when the Holy Spirit was poured out upon it. One of those changes, as has already been said, was the transition from nationalism to universalism. Another change, closely related to that one, was the separation of church and state. In the old dispensation church and state, although not identified, were intimately allied. Israel was a theocracy, one might say a church-state. Now that the church became universal, it had to be severed from the Jewish state. Just that occurred. And that is a way of saying that at Pentecost the church acquired its own distinct organization. It is not amiss to assert that, although Pentecost does not mark the birthday of the Christian church as such, it does mark the birthday of the New Testament organization of the church. It was the church in that sense which was empowered by the Holy Spirit to witness for Christ 'in Jerusalem, and in all Judea, and in Samaria, and unto the uttermost part of the earth' (Acts 1:8).

There was an organized church at Antioch in Syria. It was commanded by the Holy Spirit: 'Separate me Barnabas and Saul for the work whereunto I have called them.' The church obeyed. Significantly, it is said that Barnabas and Saul were sent out as missionaries by both the church and the Holy Spirit. 'When they had fasted and prayed, and laid their hands on them, they sent them away. So they, being sent forth by the Holy Ghost, departed' (Acts 13:2–4). In short, Saul and Barnabas were ordained divinely and ecclesiastically as missionaries.

The foregoing evidence is incontrovertible. That the church as an organization is a God-appointed agent of evangelism must be recorded as an established fact. Hence its officers must engage in evangelism, ordain missionaries, and send forth labourers into the harvest. However, it does not follow that only its officers are to be active in evangelism. Under their auspices, guidance, and control church members generally are in duty bound to bring the gospel to the unsaved.

Something must here be said concerning the Scriptural usage of the term *evangelist*. It occurs just three times in the New Testament. In Acts 21:8 Philip is called 'the evangelist'. Ephesians 4:11 reads: 'And he gave some, apostles; and some, prophets; and some, evangelists; and some, pastors and teachers.' In II Timothy 4:5 Paul admonished his spiritual son: 'Do the work of an evangelist.' In the light of these passages certain conclusions appear warranted.

The evangelist did not hold a fourth office in the apostolic church in addition to the three offices of ruling elder, teaching elder, and deacon. That would seem to be a foregone conclusion, for Christ, the Head of the church, holds the threefold office of king, prophet, and priest, and the aforenamed ecclesiastical offices represent Him in that threefold office. A fourth office in the church, co-ordinate with the three, is hardly imaginable. That conclusion is confirmed by the fact that Philip, the evangelist, was a deacon (Acts 6:5) and Timothy, the evangelist, no doubt, an elder (I Tim. 4:14; I Thess. 3:2). It is unlikely that either of them, by virtue of his being an evangelist, held a second office.

Evidently the name *evangelist* was sometimes given to men who served as itinerant preachers. Having preached the gospel in one place, they would soon move on to another. In quick succession Philip was led by the Spirit to preach at Samaria, on the road from Jerusalem to Gaza, and in Azotus (Acts 8:5, 26, 40). Thus the evangelist, on departing from a given locality, would make room for a pastor or teacher. That may be one reason why pastors and teachers are named immediately after evangelists in Ephesians 4:11.

The fact that in Ephesians 4:11 the function of evangelists is wedged in between the temporary functions of apostles and prophets and the permanent functions of pastors and teachers gives rise to the question whether evangelists were intended to serve only the apostolic church or were meant for the church of succeeding ages as well. The answer is not difficult to find. The evangelists exercised extraordinary authority, closely akin to that of the apostles. They could authoritatively appoint elders (Titus 1:5) and as individuals exercise discipline (Titus 3:10). Evidently the evangelists received special authority from the apostles, with whom they were intimately associated. It could be said that they were deputy apostles. And that can only mean that their position in the church, like the apostolic office, was a temporary one.

Whether the term *evangelist* may not be employed by the church today is quite another matter. To draw that conclusion could betray an unhealthy biblicism. True, at present the church no longer has evangelists in the specific and special sense which was in vogue in the apostolic church. But that is not a compelling reason for the avoidance of the name. Those ordained preachers, for example, who are sent out by the organized church to bring the gospel particularly to the unsaved may well be thus named. To withhold the name from unordained evangelistic workers need not be deemed a demand of principle. And, as will be shown presently, it is proper to assert that in a real sense every believer is in sacred duty bound to be an evangelist.

The subject just dealt with is one of relatively minor importance. A decidedly major matter remains to be considered.

Ever since the sixteenth-century Reformation, Protestantism has taught that three marks distinguish the true church from a false church. They are the sound preaching of the Word of God, the administration of the sacraments according to Christ's precepts, and the faithful exercise of ecclesiastical discipline. In view of the unqualified demand of the Word of God that the church engage in evangelism, the question arises whether a fourth mark should not be added; namely, the evangelizing of the unsaved. That matter is deserving of serious consideration. It may well be questioned whether there is a church anywhere which completely neglects evangelism. But if there be such a church, it is manifestly denying itself. To use a somewhat trite expression, evangelism belongs, not merely to the well-being of a church, but to its very being. Evangelism is of the essence of the true church. Yet, this is not to say that a fourth mark must be added to the traditional three. Rather, evangelism should be subsumed under the first and foremost mark. Sound preaching is preaching of the unadulterated Word of God, to be sure, but also of the whole Word. The church which utterly fails to evangelize the unsaved cannot be said to be proclaiming the whole counsel of God. Evangelism is part and parcel of sound preaching. The first mark of the true church could well be reworded so as to stress that truth.

Another matter of considerable moment must needs be named. Paul enjoined the evangelist Timothy: 'The things which thou hast heard of me among many witnesses, the same commit thou to faithful men, who shall be able to teach others also' (II Tim. 2:2). One implication of that behest is that the church must make provision for the training of evangelists, particularly of such as have in mind the devoting of their entire life to the presentation of the gospel to the lost. Here numerous churches are at fault. Almost every denomination has its theological school or schools for the training of ministers. The curriculum of many of these seminaries is designed mainly, almost exclusively even, to prepare men for service as pastors of established churches. Far more attention should be paid to the specific preparation of evangelists.

The Church as an Organism

The organized church is divinely instituted. God Himself is its founder. Did not the Son of God declare: 'Upon this rock I will build my church' (Matt. 16:18)? For that reason men should scrupulously beware of depriving it of its prerogatives. It has no more precious prerogative than that of evangelizing the world.

And yet, it does not follow that all evangelistic effort must be under the direct and complete control of the church as an organization. The church has another aspect. In addition to being an organization it is also an organism. As an organization it operates through its officers; as an organism it operates through its individual members.

God has instituted special offices in His church. But Scripture also teaches a universal office in which all believers participate. Every believer holds the threefold office of prophet, priest, and king. That truth is stated succinctly in I Peter 2:9, 'Ye are a chosen generation, a royal priesthood, an holy nation, a peculiar people; that ye should shew forth the praises of him who hath called you out of darkness into his marvellous light.' The church is a royalty of priests, a priesthood of kings. And it is the duty of every priest and king to proclaim the excellencies of his Saviour. That is his function as prophet.

The story of Eldad and Medad, told in Numbers 11, is as instructive as it is interesting. Moses alone could not bear the burden of judging the children of Israel as they journeyed through the desert. At God's command seventy elders were appointed to assist him. At a set time they were gathered at the tabernacle, the Spirit of God came upon them, and they prophesied. Eldad and Medad, however, although of the seventy, remained in the camp. Surprisingly, the Spirit came upon them also and they, too, prophesied. A young man ran and told Moses of this apparent irregularity. Moses' zealous servant, Joshua, the son of Nun, exclaimed: 'My lord Moses, forbid them.' What did Moses do? Did he rebuke Eldad and Medad? He did nothing of the kind Instead, he said: 'Would God that all the Lord's people were prophets, and that the Lord would put his Spirit upon them' (vs. 29). That was a prophetic wish. Centuries later the prophet Joel foretold the granting of that wish. God spoke through him: 'It shall come to pass afterward, that I will pour out my Spirit upon all flesh; and your sons and your daughters shall prophesy, your old men shall dream dreams, your young men shall see visions; and also upon the servants and upon the hand-maids in those days will I pour out my Spirit' (Joel 2:28, 29). That prophecy was fulfilled at Pentecost, when not only the apostles, but all the members of the Jerusalem church, were with one accord in one place and 'they were all filled with the Holy Ghost, and began to speak with other tongues, as the Spirit gave them utterance' (Acts 2:1, 4). It has been said correctly that Pentecost spells the universal prophethood of believers. It can just as well be said that the outpouring of the Holy Spirit rendered every member of the church an evangelist. So it was at Pentecost, and so it remains today. Every single believer is a God-ordained agent of evangelism.

And so the believer witnesses for Christ to his neighbours, to those at whose side he works in shop or store or office, to his fellow students and his teachers, to those over whom he has authority and to those who exercise authority over him. He invites his unchurched neighbours to worship services in his church, gathers their children in his home for the telling of Bible stories, and makes Christian tracts available in public places. He distributes Bibles to homes, hotels, and motels. In short, he sows the seed of the gospel wherever he can and casts the bread of the evangel on many waters. And for the doing of all that he does not ask to be authorized by the officers of his church. Christ, his

Lord, has authorized him. Yet, he does it as a member of Christ's body, the church.

What the believer may do as an individual he may also do in collaboration with other believers. Voluntary groups or associations of Christians may translate, publish, and distribute the Scriptures, convey the gospel by the production and dissemination of Christian literature, and in various and sundry ways spread the good news of salvation where it is not known.

To draw a sharp line of demarcation between the evangelistic activity of the church as an organization and evangelism as properly carried on by the church as an organism has sometimes been attempted but never with unqualified success. Prominent evangelical theologians have come to the conclusion that it is neither necessary nor possible. And yet, at least one stipulation must needs be made. Inasmuch as *the organized church* was instituted by God and *must* engage in evangelism, and *voluntary associations of Christians*, however legitimate and well intended, are of human origin and *may* engage in evangelism, the latter must ever be on their guard lest they supplant the former as an agent of evangelism.

In these days, when, generally speaking, the organized church is not held in as high esteem as it should be, not even by its own members, that warning is far from superfluous. It is not at all unusual for missions and evangelistic campaigns to be conducted by boards or committees which are independent of ecclesiastical control. Ordinarily that should not be done. Such associations have been known to send out ordained evangelists and even to ordain evangelists. Under normal conditions such practices must be judged to be quite out of order. Activities of that kind are clearly a prerogative of the organized church.

Whether conditions in a church may not become so abnormal as to justify the aforenamed procedures – that is another matter. When the Church of England neglected missions, many of its members banded themselves together in mission societies. They undertook what the church ought to have done but failed to do. When, about the middle of the nineteenth century, the established church of the Netherlands succumbed to theological liberalism, some of its members founded an organization for the conduct of orthodox missions, and that organization felt constrained to resort to the ordination of truly evangelical missionaries. When, in the first third of the present century, the Presbyterian Church in the United States of America fell under the spell of modernism, faithful men and women brought into being the Independent Board for Presbyterian Foreign Missions. Those were radical measures, justified, however, by existing emergencies, and praiseworthy, truly heroic. And yet, they must be recognized as exceptions to the rule. Before such steps are taken, everything possible should be done to persuade the organized church to perform its duty and to perform it well. And when subsequently there comes into being an organized church which is able and willing to conduct truly Christian evangelism, such measures should be discontinued.

Both the church as an organization and the church as an organism are God-ordained agents of evangelism. They may not clash with each other, for they are two aspects of the one body of Christ. Harmoniously they should labour for the hastening of the day when all nations whom He has made shall come and worship before the Lord and shall glorify His name (Ps. 86:9).

11: God and the Approach of Evangelism

ONE OFTEN HEARS IT SAID THAT THE HEATHEN are hungering and thirsting for the gospel. That statement is far too sweeping to be acceptable.

To be sure, God may conceivably grant to a pagan the grace of regeneration with a view to his accepting the gospel in faith as soon as it shall reach him. Whether that ever occurs, who can say? At any rate, no man has the right to restrict the sovereign grace of God by denying the possibility. In such a case there would be a longing for salvation on the part of one who is as yet ignorant of the evangel.

It is also true that pagans have consciences. Often their consciences accuse them of having offended deity. Then they desire reconciliation. That desire may become so strong that by way of appeasing deity they make great sacrifices. Thus many a Hindu mother has surrendered her babe to the waves of the sacred Ganges. In such instances there is a longing for salvation of a kind.

However, what is forgotten by those who glibly assert that the heathen hunger and thirst for the gospel is that only he who by the grace of the Holy Spirit has been born again is willing to be saved on God's terms as laid down in the evangel. All others find the message of salvation by grace offensive. That is what the Bible means when it says that 'Christ crucified' is 'unto the Jews a stumbling block, and unto the Greeks foolishness' (I Cor. 1:23). So great is the depravity of unregenerate man that, although there is nothing that he needs more than the gospel, there is nothing that he desires less.

It follows that, when considering the approach of evangelism, one may not suppose that there is in the natural man some spiritual good which renders his heart fertile soil for the seed of the gospel. Only when the Holy Spirit has given him a heart of flesh for one of stone (Ezek. 11:19) will the seed fall into good ground and bring forth the fruit of faith (Matt. 13:8, 23).

In what sense, then, may one speak of the approach of evangelism? What follows is an answer to that question.

The Religious Nature of Man

Man was created in the image and after the likeness of God (Gen. 1:26). That distinguishes man from all other earthly creatures. It is that which makes man to be man. One aspect of the divine image in man is what theologians term *sensus deitatis*, a sense of deity. Man is aware of the existence of a supreme being. It has been said that man is incurably religious. Religion not being a disease, it is much better to say that man is *constitutionally* religious.

When man fell into sin, the image of God in him suffered incalculable injury. Yet it was not completely obliterated. Vestiges of it remain. Fallen man is still a human being. But the gifts which God bestowed upon him in the beginning and which he once used to the glory of God he now employs in opposition to God, for instead of loving God he now hates him (Rom. 1:30). That, in brief, is the doctrine of total depravity.

Prominent among the aspects of the divine image which fallen man has retained is his *sensus deitatis*. To be sure, also that gift he has utterly corrupted. He has 'exchanged

[129]

the truth of God for a lie, and worshipped and served the creature rather than the Creator' (Rom. 1:25 ASV). Nevertheless he still possesses a religious nature. That is true of every human being, the most blatant 'atheist' included. There was much more than a modicum of truth in the saying so often repeated during the second world war, 'There are no atheists in foxholes.' To the point is the story of the man who vowed violently that he believed neither in God nor in immortality but, when facing execution for murder, prayed: 'O God, if there be a God, save my soul, if I have a soul.' In the darkest parts of the dark continent of Africa no tribe was ever found devoid of religion. Atheistic communism is itself a religion. It worships the state.

Perverted though it is, man's religious nature can serve as a point of contact for him who brings the gospel to the lost. The missionary Paul made such use of it in pagan Athens. Said he to the Areopagus, the high court of the Athenians: 'Men of Athens, I perceive that in every way you are very religious. For as I passed along, and observed the objects of your worship, I found also an altar with this inscription, "To an unknown god". What therefore you worship as unknown, this I proclaim to you' (Acts 17:22, 23 RSV). It must be noted that both the American Standard Version and the Revised Standard Version have at this point corrected a rather obvious mistranslation in the King James Version. The Greek adjective *deisidaimōn*, the comparative degree of which is here used, may mean either *religious* or *superstitious*. But it is not at all likely that in the opening sentence of his address Paul would have charged his hearers with being *too superstitious*. To have done so would seem almost unbelievably tactless. Nor is it complimentary to the apostle to suppose, as some do, that he resorted to a kindly ambiguity. Beyond all reasonable doubt, he meant to tell his Athenian hearers that he had observed them to be *very religious*.

Truth in False Religions

In recent decades scholars have given much attention to the Science of Religion. Under that head fall the History of Religion, which aims to collect and arrange historical facts; Comparative Religion, which compares religions with one another in the light of those facts; and the Psychology or Philosophy of Religion, which generalizes, especially as to the origin of religion, on the basis of those facts. Sometimes all three of these are subsumed under the head History of Religion or Religions.

The History of Religion seeks to answer the question, among others, how religion originated. But obviously this cannot be determined on a historical basis. Religion originated in pre-historic times. Therefore historians have been compelled to adopt psychological explanations of the origin of religion. For instance, it has been said that from reverence for the head of a tribe or from fear of the superhuman forces of nature early man deduced the concept of a supreme being. Admittedly, that is guesswork. The only way in which we can gain sure knowledge of the pre-historic is by revelation from God. Either we must accept the Scriptural account of the origin of religion or resign ourselves to uncertainty.

As to the origin and history of religion there are two widely divergent, even opposite, schools of thought. They may be denominated naturalistic or evolutionistic and supernaturalistic or revelational. The former teaches that primitive man of his own initiative arrived at a crude concept of God and that in the course of history through human reflection and experience that concept was gradually purified and ennobled. Monotheism, for example, is said to be a relatively late development. The book Deuteronomy, which insists uncompromisingly that there is but one God (Deut. 6:4), cannot, we are told, have been written by Moses; it must have come into being several centuries later. The great majority of modern writers on the History of Religion take that position, a notable exception being Roman Catholic Wilhelm Schmidt of the University of Vienna, who in his monumental work *The Origin of the Idea of God* claims that by the historical method he has come to the conclusion that the earliest religion of man was monotheistic and that the history of the ethnic religions is one of degradation instead of evolution.

As to the teaching of Scripture on this matter, there can be no doubt. The first man, created as he was in the image of the Creator, possessed true knowledge of God as well as righteousness and holiness (Col. 3:10; Eph. 4:24). Only when he fell into sin was his knowledge of God corrupted and his attitude to God perverted. And only through special revelation, supernaturally given, is true religion restored.

Let no one draw the conclusion that today all religions other than Christianity are utterly false. That does not follow. To be sure, they are *essentially* false, and Christianity is the one true religion. More will be said on that subject at another point in this study. Suffice it now to say that all other religions are false in that they teach false gods and false ways of salvation. Yet, the fact that all the religions of the world are corruptions of the original true religion goes a long way toward accounting for elements of truth in those religions. It would have been surpassing strange if every shred of truth had disappeared from them.

We know that as a matter of fact God did not permit that to occur.

And so we find that all religions have two beliefs in common: belief in a supreme being and belief in the immortality of man. To that may be added that they also have two practices in common: prayer and the bringing of offerings. Christianity, too, has those beliefs and practices, and Christianity possesses them in their pure form, while in all other religions they are grossly corrupted. For a concrete example, not even the monotheism of Judaism is to be identified with the monotheism of Christianity, for Judaistic monotheism leaves no room for the Triune God of the Bible and Christianity. Nevertheless, in one form or another the aforenamed beliefs and practices persist in the many religions of mankind.

The Bible records a striking instance of Paul's use of an element of truth in a false religion as a point of contact in evangelism. It happened at Athens. The apostle told the Areopagites that God is 'not far from every one of us: for in him we live, and move, and have our being; as certain also of your own poets have said, For we are also his offspring.' He was quoting verbatim Aratus of Soli in Cilicia, a poet of the third century B.C., and almost verbatim Cleanthes of Assos in Mysia, a disciple of the philosopher Zeno. Then, having expressed his agreement with these pagan poets, Paul proceeded to berate the Athenians for their idolatry. Said he: 'Forasmuch then as we are the offspring of God, we ought not to think that the Godhead is like unto gold, or silver, or stone, graven by art and man's device' (Acts 17:27-29). All the more remarkable was the approach here employed by Paul if it be remembered that his exegesis of the statement, 'For we are also his offspring' must have differed greatly from that of Aratus and Cleanthes. But he did find a truth, however much perverted, in a pagan religion, and he made it his starting point in the proclamation of the only true God.

The Common Grace of God

The Bible teaches emphatically that the goodness, even the love, of God extends to all His rational creatures. 'The Lord is gracious, and full of compassion; slow to anger and of great mercy. The Lord is good to all'; so sang the Psalmist (Ps. 145:8, 9). With an eye to God's compassion on wicked Nineveh, Jonah testified: 'I knew that thou art a gracious God, and merciful, slow to anger, and of great kindness, and repentest thee of the evil' (Jonah 4:2). The Lord Jesus commanded His disciples: 'Love your enemies, bless them that curse you, do good to them that hate you, and pray for them which despitefully use you and persecute you; that ye may be the children of your Father which is in heaven: for he maketh his sun to rise on the evil and on the good, and sendeth rain on the just and on the unjust' (Matt. 5:44, 45).

That the greatest of all Christian missionaries used the common grace of God as a point of departure in the proclamation of the saving grace of God is worthy of note. He told the people of Lystra and Derbe that the living God 'left not himself without witness, in that he did good, and gave us rain from heaven, and fruitful seasons, filling our hearts with food and gladness' (Acts 14:17).

The blessings of nature poured out on all mankind are but one evidence of the common grace of God. The restraint of sin in the lives of the wicked and the virtues exercised by the unregenerate are additional evidences. That, as was previously pointed out, vestiges of the divine image remain in fallen man and that not every trace of truth has vanished from the ethnic religions is due to the goodness of God. That even sinners, unregenerate men, do good of a kind (Luke 6:32, 33) is to be explained in no other way. The respect with which the Chinese are wont to regard their progenitors, even though it has degenerated into abominable worship of ancestors, is a good which affords to the Christian missionary a point of contact. What missionary among Jews or Mohammedans would not turn to advantage their monotheism, stark and sterile though it is? Islamic fatalism, too, while very far removed from the Christian doctrine of divine foreordination, contains enough truth to be of some use to him who would evangelize Moslems.

God's Revelation in Nature

Both the natural and the spiritual are divine creations. They also have this in common that both reveal the Creator. Small wonder that they are analogous one to the other. That could hardly be otherwise.

It is well to bear in mind that the natural is patterned after the spiritual, not the spiritual after the natural. The fact that all nature is a revelation of God, who is 'spirit' (John 4:24 RSV), leaves room for no other possibility. When Jesus spoke of Himself as 'the true vine' (John 15:1), He meant to teach that He is the original, the archetypal, vine and that the grape-vine was made to resemble Him. The reason why Scripture speaks of God as Father is not that He somewhat resembles fathers among men, but human fathers are so called because they remotely resemble God. God's fatherhood is from eternity. Before human fatherhood was, God is Father. Henry Drummond's book *Natural Law in the Spiritual World* had better been entitled *Spiritual Law in the Natural World*.

In His teaching the Lord Jesus was keenly aware of the analogy of the natural to the spiritual. He often taught in parables. What is a parable but an earthly story with a heavenly meaning, a natural story with a spiritual meaning? While each of Jesus' parables teaches its own lesson, all His parables together convey one lesson: that the natural and the spiritual, revelations as they are of the one God, are analogous to each other.

In his evangelism the Saviour freely used the natural as an approach. Under the figure of birth He introduced to Nicodemus the subject of entrance into the kingdom of God (John 3:3–6). When He saw the Samaritan woman coming toward Jacob's well with a cruse on her shoulder, He asked her for a drink of water, ordinary water, before recommending to her that living water, whereof if one drinks, he will nevermore thirst (John 4:7–14). After bidding the paralytic at the pool Bethesda to take up his bed and walk and enabling him to obey, He sought him out to tell him: 'Behold, thou art made whole: sin no more, lest a worse thing come unto thee' (John 5:1–14). By healing another paralytic He proved that He had power to forgive sins (Mark 2:1–12). He first opened the eyes of the man who was born blind and then bestowed upon him the spiritual sight of faith (John 9:1–38). All His miracles of healing were symbolic of spiritual healing. And by raising the dead He taught men that His was the divine prerogative to bring to life those who are dead in trespasses and sins.

The task of the evangelist is spiritual. He must bring to the lost the gospel of salvation from sin and spiritual death. He may permit nothing to deflect him from the accomplishment of that mission. Yet, if he is wise, his approach to those whom he would evangelize will be natural. To do so will be highly conducive to the proper performance of his task. They err who hold that it is out of place for him to show concern about the physical well-being of those whose souls he would win for Christ. Precisely that is what he ought to do. He should manifest a warm interest in their health, their crops, their trades, their livelihood. Above all else, he should make friends of their children, for there is no human instinct stronger than the love of parents for their offspring. Can anyone doubt that, when Jesus embraced infants, blessed them, and spoke: 'Suffer the little children to come unto me, and forbid them not; for of such is the kingdom of God' (Mark 10:14), He had in mind to lead their mothers also into the kingdom?

Missionary Adaptation

That the missionary must adjust himself to those whom he would evangelize need hardly be said. That he must make the necessary adjustments without the sacrifice of principles is just as clear. The missionary Paul put both those rules into practice in masterful fashion.

When the evangelist Timothy was to accompany him on a tour of Asia Minor, Paul 'took and circumcised him because of the Jews which were in those quarters; for they knew all that his father was a Greek' (Acts 16:3). On the other hand, when Judaizers demanded that the evangelist Titus be circumcised, the same apostle 'gave place by subjection, no, not for an hour' (Gal. 2:3–5). There was no inconsistency here. In one instance, no principle being at stake, a course of expediency was followed; in the other instance the truth of salvation by grace and the principle of Christian liberty had to be upheld.

There are various opinions as to why Christ's chosen missionary to the gentiles changed his name from Saul, Hebrew for *asked*, to Paul, Greek for *little*. Some think that the change was occasioned by his conversion and was intended as an expression of humility. Others incline to the view that the apostle named himself after Sergius Paulus, governor of Cyprus, the first recorded convert of his first missionary journey. As a matter of fact, in relating the story of this conversion the historian Luke for the first time spoke of Saul as Paul (Acts 13:9). But it seems more likely that the change of name was a mere matter of missionary adaptation. Now that he was sent forth to carry the evangel to the gentile world, he thought it more advisable to go by a Greek name than a Hebrew.

Some think that Paul went beyond the bounds of proper adaptation when, having returned to Jerusalem from his third missionary journey, he followed the advice of his friends to take a ceremonial vow in order to prove to Jewish believers that he had not broken with all Jewish traditions (Acts 21:20-25). True it is that the taking of that vow got him into exceedingly serious trouble. However, whether or not he erred in this matter is difficult to determine. This writer prefers to give the missionary-apostle the benefit of the doubt.

The apostolic church confronted a problem which is a bone of contention on many a mission field today. What was to be done about pagan polygamists on their conversion to Christianity? Was the dismissal of all their wives save one to be a condition of reception into church membership? The New Testament answers that question. Titus 1:6 and I Timothy 3:2, 12 laid down the rule that both elders and deacons had to be 'the husband of one wife'. This cannot mean that they had to be married. If Paul had meant that, he would have said it, and no mention would have been made of *one* wife. Nor is it at all likely that the apostle barred from office in the church the man who had entered upon a second marriage after the death of his first wife. Elsewhere the same apostle taught: 'The woman which hath an husband is bound by the law to her husband; but if the husband be dead, she is loosed from the law of her husband. So then if, while her husband liveth, she be married to another man, she shall be called an adulteress; but if her husband be dead, she is free from that law; so that she is no adulteress, though she be married to another man' (Rom. 7:2, 3). Surely, that holds for husbands as well as wives. Beyond reasonable doubt, although the New Testament in no way sanctions, or even condones, polygamy, and no member of the apostolic church was permitted to enter upon a multiple marriage, yet, by way of concession a convert with more wives than one was sometimes received into church membership. In no case, however, was such a member to aspire, or be chosen, to office in the church. That concession may have been made because the polygamist's dismissal of all his wives save one could easily create more problems than it would solve and could do more moral harm than good. Besides, that concession was, of course, an exceptional measure. Nor does it necessarily follow that precisely the same concession should today be made on every single mission field where a more or less similar situation obtains. Much depends on the precise circumstances in a given field.

Paul has given emphatic expression to his willingness to accommodate himself to those whom he sought to win for Christ. Said he: 'Though I be free from all men, yet have I made myself servant unto all, that I might gain the more. And unto the Jews became I as a Jew, that I might gain the

Jews; to them that are under the law, as under the law, that I might gain them that are under the law; to them that are without law, as without law (being not without law to God, but under the law to Christ), that I might gain them that are without law. To the weak became I as weak, that I might gain the weak: I am made all things to all men, that I might by all means save some' (I Cor. 9: 19–22).

And what can be said of the matchless condescension of the Saviour Himself? Here such terms as *adaptation, accommodation,* and *adjustment* must be rejected as utterly inadequate. He who was 'holy, harmless, undefiled, separate from sinners, and made higher than the heavens' (Heb. 7: 26) received sinners and ate with them (Luke 15: 2). He who as the Son of man received from the Ancient of days 'dominion, and glory, and a kingdom, that all people, nations, and languages should serve him' and whose dominion is 'an everlasting dominion, which shall not pass away' (Dan. 7: 13, 14), roamed about 'to seek and to save that which was lost' (Luke 19: 10) and came 'not to be ministered unto but to minister', even 'to give his life a ransom for many' (Matt. 20: 28). He who was very God 'counted not the being on an equality with God a thing to be grasped, but emptied himself', not, to be sure, of His divine nature, yet of His glory. He 'made himself of no reputation, and took upon him the form of a servant, and was made in the likeness of men: and being found in fashion as a man, he humbled himself, and became obedient unto death, even the death of the cross' (Phil. 2: 7, 8).

12: God and the Means of Evangelism

CHRISTIAN THEOLOGY SPEAKS OF MEANS OF grace. God is pleased to employ means in bringing sinners to faith, and He also employs means in building up saints in the faith. In the former instance, the means is the Word of God; in the latter the means are the Word of God and the divinely instituted sacraments.

Faith and the Word of God

It is a matter of supreme importance to maintain that the Word of God is the one and only indispensable means by which the Holy Spirit works faith in the hearts of men. Although this does not mean that the Word always operates in isolation from every other conceivable factor, another factor never serves as a substitute for the Word. At most it is only auxiliary and subsidiary to the Word.

The gist of the Great Commission is that men of every nation are to be made disciples of Christ by being taught the Word of God.

It hardly needs to be pointed out in detail that in the apostolic age evangelism was performed by the teaching and preaching of the Word. That was invariably the case. Wholly of course, evangelism is the bringing of the evangel, and the evangel is the Word of God. Romans 10:13–17 states the case in summary fashion. After asserting: 'Whosoever shall call on the name of the Lord shall be saved', the inspired writer proceeds: 'How then shall they call on him in whom they have not believed? and how shall they believe in him of whom they have not heard? and how shall they hear without a preacher? and how shall they preach except they be sent? as it is written, How beautiful are the feet of them that preach the gospel of peace, and bring glad tidings of good things! . . . So then faith cometh by hearing, and hearing by the Word of God.' The task of the evangelist is to confront men with the Word of God.

Knowledge of the Word of God is a prerequisite of saving faith. More than that, it is a constitutive element of saving faith. The believer consents to the truth revealed in the Word of God and entrusts himself for salvation to the Son of God, but manifestly he can do neither of these without knowledge of the content of Scripture. They err grievously who put a premium on ignorance by suggesting that the less knowledge one has of the Bible, the simpler and stronger one's faith is going to be. The antithesis of knowledge and faith is utterly false. Faith is neither a leap in the dark nor a gamble. Every one who commits himself to the Saviour does so because of his knowledge of the Saviour, gained from Holy Writ.

To the question how much knowledge the evangelist is to require of him who by profession of faith would unite with Christ's church there is no hard-and-fast answer, but it is safe to say that he must know that Jesus is the Christ, the Son of God, the one and only Saviour by His substitutionary death, and Lord of all. It may also be said without hesitation that he who is to be baptized into the name of the Father, the Son, and the Holy Spirit must have some knowledge of the Triune God. And *The Apostles' Creed* being an elaboration of the doctrine of the Trinity, he may justly be expected to subscribe to the basic teachings of the Christian religion as contained in that ecumenical confession. As to himself, he must know that he is a sinner who needs salvation, that he cannot possibly save himself, and that salvation is by the grace of the Triune God. The abandonment of himself to that grace is the essence of saving faith.

A distinction has been made between the acceptance of the Scriptural *propositions* concerning Christ and the committing of oneself to the *person* of Christ. The distinction is valid. Conceivably, one may accept such propositions as that Christ was born of the virgin Mary, that He died for sinners on Calvary's cross, and that He arose from the dead, and yet not commit oneself for salvation to the person of Christ. Then one has only so-called speculative or historical faith, such as Paul ascribed to king Agrippa when he asked him whether he believed the prophets and immediately added: 'I know that thou believest' (Acts 26:27). It is a case of orthodoxism or dead orthodoxy. However, let no one harbour the thought for so much as a moment that it is possible to believe on the person of Christ without believing what the Bible teaches concerning Him. That is entirely out of the question.

Not infrequently evangelists, when demanding of sinners that they believe in Christ, confuse the essence of faith with the full assurance of faith. That is a serious blunder. While a measure of assurance invariably accompanies saving faith, in fact is inherent in it, one may very well possess the essence of saving faith without always enjoying complete assurance. One may not be able to say every hour of the day: 'I know that my Redeemer liveth' (Job 19:25) and 'I know whom I have believed' (II Tim. 1:12), and yet be a true believer. Therefore the evangelist ought not to insist that a candidate for Christian baptism be unqualifiedly certain that Christ died to save him and that he is now on the road to everlasting glory. He should ask no more than what Paul required of the Philippian jailer: 'Believe on the Lord Jesus Christ' (Acts 16:31). To look away from self for salvation and to look to the crucified Christ, as the Israelites, bitten by venomous serpents, looked to the brazen serpent, that is saving faith (John 3:14, 15). Evidently Naaman, the Syrian, had precious little assurance when he waded into Jordan, but his doing so was proof of his faith, and by that faith, however small and weak, he was cleansed of his leprosy (II Kings 5:1–14). Jesus equated faith in Him with coming to Him when He said: 'He that cometh to me shall never hunger; and he that believeth on me shall never thirst' (John 6:35). Fleeing for salvation to the Christ of the Word is itself an act of faith.

The Word of God and Exemplary Conduct

No one has the right to say that God cannot use His Word unto the salvation of sinners if that Word is brought by an unsaved person. God is sovereign, and also at this point His sovereignty must be respected. He put a wonderfully beautiful Messianic prophecy into the mouth of ungodly Balaam (Num. 24:17–19) and had wicked Caiaphas testify of Christ's vicarious atonement (John 11:49–51). Judas Iscariot was one of the twelve sent out by Jesus to preach the gospel. God may employ unto the salvation of souls the gospel of truth spoken by an infidel or a hypocrite.

However, he who teaches the Word of God to others and is not himself a doer thereof has no right to expect the divine blessing to rest upon his teaching. What he does contradicts what he says. Men have every reason to chide him, 'Physician, heal thyself', and to cast into his teeth the saying, trite though it is, 'What you do speaks so loud that I cannot hear what you say.' He may well give heed to Ophelia's cutting advice in Shakespeare's *Hamlet* to her brother Laertes:

> Do not, as some ungracious pastors do,
> Show me the steep and thorny way to heaven:
> Whilst like a puff'd and reckless libertine
> Himself the primrose path of dalliance treads,
> And recks not his own rede.

On the other hand, the life of the godly evangelist will reinforce his message by witnessing eloquently to its truth. In the prologue to his *Canterbury Tales* Chaucer sang the praises of such a bearer of the gospel in the lines:

> A good man was ther of religioun
> And was a povre Persoun of a toun;
> But riche he was of holy thoght and werk.
> He was also a lerned man, a clerk,
> That Cristes gospel trewely wolde preche;
> His parisshens devoutly wolde he teche.
> He wayted after no pompe and reverence,
> Ne maked him a spyced conscience,
> But Cristes lore, and his apostles twelve,
> He taught, but first he folwed it himselve.

Let no one conclude that a godly life and exemplary behaviour may take the place of the evangel and render it superfluous. That position is often taken, and not infrequently a story from the life of Francis of Assisi is piously used to support it. One day Francis invited a youthful monk to accompany him to a certain village with the intent of preaching the gospel. On arriving at the village, they found much poverty and disease. The alleviation of that misery kept them busy the livelong day. Toward evening the young monk turned to Francis with the troubled question as to when they were going to begin to preach. Francis replied: 'We have been preaching the gospel all day.' If Francis meant to equate deeds of mercy with the Word of God as a means of grace, he was mistaken.

Those who hold that an example of godliness may be substituted for the evangel are not on Biblical ground. When Jesus sent forth His twelve apostles to the lost sheep of the house of Israel, He charged them: 'Preach, saying, The kingdom of heaven is at hand. Heal the sick' (Matt. 10: 7, 8). They were not merely to heal but also to preach. In fact, preaching was their first and primary task. They obeyed and 'went through the towns, preaching the gospel and healing every where' (Luke 9: 6). Anyone at all familiar with Paul's missionary career will know that he regarded preaching as his calling and made healing subsidiary to it.

There is a passage of Scripture which at first blush seems to teach that in some instances the Word of God may be ignored in evangelism and exemplary behaviour may take its place. The apostle Peter exhorted the wives of unbelieving husbands: 'Ye wives, be in subjection to your own husbands; that, if any obey not the word, they also may without the word be won by the conversation of the wives; while they behold your chaste conversation coupled with fear' (I Peter 3: 1, 2). It may be observed that it is almost inconceivable that the unbelieving spouse of a Christian woman would have no acquaintance whatever with the Word of God. But another consideration is of even greater weight. The rendering 'without the word' is faulty. In the original the definite article is lacking. Therefore the translation 'without a word' of the Revised Standard Version is correct. The reference of the phrase, then, is not to the Word of God but to the word of the woman concerned. Popularly put, by her walk rather than her talk she must seek to win her unbelieving husband for Christ.

Nor does II Corinthians 3:3 teach that the Christian life is a fitting substitute for the Christian gospel. The verse reads: 'Forasmuch as ye are manifestly declared to be the epistle of Christ ministered by us, written not with ink, but with the Spirit of the living God; not in tables of stone, but in fleshy tables of the heart.' This passage has been interpreted to mean that the life of each believer is a Spirit-written version of the gospel of Christ. In the light of the context that construction cannot stand. Paul was being maligned in Corinth. Even within the church some questioned his apostleship. With that in mind he asked: 'Need we . . . epistles of commendation to you, or letters of commendation from you?' He himself answered that question: 'Ye are our epistle written in our hearts, known and read of all men' (II Cor. 3:1, 2). Then, enlarging on the concept *epistle*, he went on to say in effect: 'You Corinthian believers in your Christian condition are manifestly a letter which Christ has caused to be written through me and my fellow-labourers in the gospel by the operation of the Holy Spirit in your hearts.' The epistle spoken of was Paul's letter of recommendation. The Corinthian Christians were that letter. By rendering them Christians through Paul's preaching and its application to their hearts by the Holy Spirit, Christ recommended Paul as His apostle. Parallel to this passage is Paul's statement, also addressed to the believers at Corinth: 'The seal of mine apostleship are ye in the Lord' (I Cor. 9:2). But to identify

[147]

'the epistle of Christ' with the gospel is quite beside the point.

It is clear that, while the evangelist is in sacred duty bound to reinforce his message with exemplary Christian conduct, godly living is not a substitute for the gospel.

The Word of God and Religious Experience

Experience is of the essence of Christianity. The new birth, without which no man can see the kingdom of God (John 3:3), is an experience, albeit a subconscious one. Conviction of sin, repentance toward God, faith in Christ, growth in holiness, are all of them conscious experiences and as necessary as is regeneration.

Yet, the substitution of religious experience, whether of the evangelist or of the evangelized, for the gospel is a most serious error. It is also a rampant error.

In the second half of the eighteenth century preaching in Germany had, by and large, fallen under the spell of rationalism. Scriptural teachings that were thought not to square with human reason, such as the doctrines of original sin, the substitutionary atonement, and justification by faith, were banished from the pulpit. Such doctrines as that of the Holy Trinity and the two natures of Christ were pronounced purely speculative. From this rationalism the beginning of the nineteenth century brought a reaction under the leadership of Friedrich D. E. Schleiermacher of the University of Berlin, and this reaction has ever since exerted a mighty influence on preaching throughout Christendom.

Sad to say, Schleiermacher's reaction from rationalism was vitiated by his faulty view of Scripture. He regarded the Bible, not as God's objective revelation of Himself to man, but as a record of the subjective religious experience of outstanding saints. In consequence, he argued that the content of preaching must be derived from the religious consciousness of the preacher, to be identified with the religious consciousness of the congregation and nourished by the reading of Scripture, especially the New Testament. According to Schleiermacher preaching is not the explanation and application of Scripture, but the imparting of the religious consciousness, and the aim of preaching is not indoctrination, but Christian living. Thus Schleiermacher agreed with rationalism that the content of preaching is to be obtained subjectively, but in distinction from rationalism he took as his starting point, not the rational, but the religious subject.

The famous Berlin theologian is known as the father of present-day theological liberalism. Due to his influence, liberal preaching of our day has substituted subjective religious experience for the objective Word of God. That holds of liberal evangelism, too. And regrettably, not all evangelical or fundamentalist evangelism is completely free of that blight.

That such slighting of the Word of God in evangelism is unscriptural requires no proof. To say so is an understatement. It is antiscriptural. It constitutes a flagrant flouting of Paul's solemn command to his spiritual son and his associate in evangelism: 'I charge thee therefore before God, and the Lord Jesus Christ, who shall judge the quick and the dead at his appearing and his kingdom: preach the Word; be instant in season, out of season; reprove, rebuke, exhort with all long-suffering and doctrine' (I Tim. 4: 1, 2). It amounts to a blatant denial of the affirmation: 'The Word of God is quick, and powerful, and sharper than any two-edged sword, piercing even to the dividing asunder of soul and spirit, and of the joints and marrow, and is a discerner of the thoughts and intents of the heart' (Heb. 4: 12).

The view is widely held and frequently expressed that men are sometimes brought into the kingdom by a more or less startling experience, with little or no reference to the Word of God. For instance, sinners are said to have been converted through a serious illness, as the result of a well-nigh fatal accident, or by the death of a beloved child.

Although it must ever be maintained that the new birth is prerequisite to the exercise of saving faith, it need not be denied that God may employ such experiences to prepare sinners psychologically for the reception of the gospel. But that such experiences are another means of grace in addition to the Word of God, or in its place, must be denied vigorously.

The teaching of Jesus on the point at issue is most clear. In the parable of the rich man and Lazarus, Dives, suffering the torments of hell, is said to see Abraham afar off, and Lazarus in his bosom. When his request that Lazarus be sent to cool his tongue by placing on it a finger dipped in water has been refused, he makes a supremely urgent plea: 'I pray thee, therefore, father, that thou wouldest send him to my father's house; for I have five brethren, that he may testify unto them, lest they also come into this place of torment.' Abraham answers: 'They have Moses and the prophets; let them hear them.' Dives insists: 'Nay, father Abraham; but if one went unto them from the dead, they will repent.' Abraham's reply is categorical: 'If they hear not Moses and the prophets, neither will they be persuaded, though one rose from the dead' (Luke 16: 23–31). 'Moses and the prophets' were the Bible of that day. It is difficult to imagine an experience more startling than a visit by one risen from the dead. The most impressive experience will not save him who refuses to heed the Word of God.

The Word of God and Prayer

Prayer is sometimes spoken of as a means of grace. It may be so regarded if it be remembered that prayer is not as a means of grace to be equated with the Word of God, nor even to be co-ordinated with it. The Word of God and prayer are means of grace in differing senses. God imparts saving grace through the instrumentality of His Word. He frequently imparts saving grace in answer to prayer.

Two brief statements may here be made which ought to be quite superfluous, but perhaps are not. Their truth seems not to be self-evident to all.

To pray, however fervently, for the conversion of the unsaved, whether they be in China or in the house next door, and to take no action whatever toward acquainting them with the gospel of Jesus Christ, is an abomination.

To be never so diligent in bringing the evangel to the lost, and not to pray that God may bless the evangel to their hearts unto salvation, is the height of folly, for only God the Holy Spirit can effectually by the Word call sinners to repentance.

13: God and the Message of Evangelism

THE MESSAGE OF EVANGELISM IS SO BROAD A theme that a large volume could hardly do it justice. This chapter will be restricted to the consideration of its God-centred character, and admittedly the treatment of that one phase will be far from exhaustive.

Let it be said at the outset that the evangel is as Christ-centred as it is God-centred. Those terms are synonymous. To be sure, that does not apply to the Christ of modern theology, according to which Jesus of Nazareth was divine only in the sense in which all men are divine, with the difference that the spark of divinity burned more brightly in Him than it does in any other human being. But it does apply to the Christ of Scripture, who is the highest revelation of God and is Himself God of God. 'Being the effulgence of his glory and the very image of his substance' (Heb. 1:3 ASV), he could declare: 'He that hath seen me hath seen the Father' (John 14:9) and 'I and my Father are one' (John 10:30).

The Gospel of Repentance

The Bible often speaks of the evangel as the gospel of repentance. For instance, John the Baptist preached 'the baptism of repentance for the remission of sins' (Mark 1:4) and, when John had been imprisoned, Jesus came into Galilee, preaching the gospel of the kingdom of God and saying: 'Repent ye, and believe the gospel' (Mark 1:15).

For a compelling reason the call to repentance must

come first in evangelism. Only he who is oppressed by sin will realize his need of the Saviour. Only he who knows himself to be guilty and foul will run to Calvary for pardon and cleansing. Some present-day psychiatrists to the contrary notwithstanding, conviction of sin is an indispensable prerequisite of faith in Christ.

In order that sinners may be brought to repentance, the law of God, which is 'holy, and just, and good' (Rom. 7:12), as God Himself is, must be preached, for 'by the law is the knowledge of sin' (Rom. 3:20). He who views himself in that perfect mirror can only abhor himself.

Two kinds of sorrow for sin lie far apart. Paul wrote: 'Godly sorrow worketh repentance to salvation not to be repented of: but the sorrow of the world worketh death' (II Cor. 7:10). Calvin has commented: 'The sorrow of the world is, when men despond in consequence of earthly afflictions, and are overwhelmed with grief; while sorrow according to God is that which has an eye to God, while they reckon it the *one* misery to have lost the favour of God.' The one springs solely from love of self and leads deathward; the other is rooted in reverence for God and results in repentance unto salvation.

There is a great difference between repentance and remorse. When Judas Iscariot had betrayed the Lord, he was overwhelmed by remorse and hanged himself (Matt. 27:5). When Simon Peter had denied the Lord, he wept bitter tears of repentance (Matt. 26:75). The remorseful sinner hastens from Christ; the penitent flees to him.

A popular notion, which the evangelist must take pains to dispel, is that true repentance can come too late. Scripture teaches the contrary. When saying that Esau 'found no place for repentance, though he sought it carefully with tears' (Heb. 12:17), the sacred writer referred to repentance on the part of Isaac, not of Esau. Esau did not succeed in causing his father Isaac to change his mind so as to recall the blessing of the birthright bestowed upon Jacob and to confer it on his elder son. In this he did not succeed although he sought it with tears. The incident, then, has no relevance to the point at issue. Another incident in Bible history bears on it most directly. The malefactor at Jesus' right hand on Calvary had sinned his life away. Only a matter of hours before his death he turned in penitence to the Saviour. Was he rejected because of his tardiness? Contrariwise, he rejoiced to hear the comforting assurance: 'Verily I say unto thee, Today shalt thou be with me in paradise' (Luke 23:43). Ere the day was spent his Saviour and he passed hand in hand through the gate of heaven, and the angels of God praised the power of the blood.

Heartfelt repentance is indispensable for salvation. Yet repentance does not merit salvation. How could it? It is itself a gift of God. When the apostle Peter reported to the saints at Jerusalem the conversion of Cornelius, they glorified God, saying: 'Then hath God also to the gentiles granted repentance unto life' (Acts 11:18). Augustus M. Toplady was right when he confessed:

> Could my tears for ever flow,
> All for sin could not atone;
> Thou must save, and Thou alone.

The Gospel of the Atonement

The heart of the gospel is not concerned with what God requires of sinners. That is indeed one aspect of the gospel and an important one, but it does not lie at the centre of the evangel. As its very name indicates, the evangel is not in its essence a command but news, good news. It is the glad tidings of what God in Christ has done for the salvation of sinners.

A criminal finds himself in prison, locked in his cell. A visiting friend calls out to him: 'I have good news for you.' With eager expectation the prisoner demands: 'What is it? Out with it!' The answer comes: 'Be good.' Well might that drive the prisoner mad. Yet, precisely that is the only message which some who call themselves evangelists have for the sinner. It is not good news. It is not news at all. Good news for the sinner is that provision has been made for his release from sin and hell.

Provision was made on Calvary. The Crucified One 'was wounded for our transgressions, he was bruised for our iniquities; the chastisement of our peace was upon him; and with his stripes are we healed. All we like sheep have gone astray; we have turned every one to his own way; and the Lord hath laid on him the iniquity of us all' (Isa. 53:5, 6). God 'hath made him to be sin for us, who knew no sin, that we might be made the righteousness of God in him' (II Cor. 5:21). From the curse of God which we had merited by not continuing in all things which are written in the book of the law He redeemed us, being made a curse for us, for it is written: 'Cursed is every one that hangeth on a tree' (Gal. 3:10, 13). The anguish and torment of very hell which we sinners have deserved swallowed Him up when He cried with a loud voice: 'My God, my God, why hast thou forsaken me?' (Matt. 27:46).

That is the story of Christ's death by crucifixion. That is also God's own interpretation of that story. Together they constitute the heart of the evangel. By His death on the cross the Son of God fully satisfied for sinners the divine penal justice.

Liberal theology has seriously distorted the Scriptural doctrine of the atonement. We are told that the death of Christ was intended to reconcile man to God but did not reconcile God to man. It is said that, God being love, there was no need of His being reconciled. True it is that the heart of God did not need to be softened by the blood of the Lamb of God as, according to an ancient legend, adamant is melted by the blood of a lamb. For God so loved the world that He gave His only begotten Son to die for its sins. But never may it be forgotten that, according to His self-revelation in Holy Writ, the God of infinite love is also a God of absolute justice and boundless wrath. At the dawn of human history the justice of God decreed that the wages of sin would be death (Gen. 2:17; Rom. 6:23), even death eternal. For God to depart a hair-breadth from the path of perfect justice would be to deny Himself. But that is the one thing which God cannot do (II Tim. 2:13). And so, rather than let sin go unpunished, He punished it by the accursed death of His own beloved Son. And by nature all men are 'the children of wrath' (Eph. 2:3). Upon those who do not believe the Son the wrath of God abides (John 3:36). On the other hand, believers, 'being now justified by his blood', are 'saved from wrath through him' (Rom. 5:9).

A supremely significant aspect of the Biblical doctrine of the atonement remains to be named. Even evangelical theologians often neglect it. Christ's 'active' obedience was as necessary for the salvation of sinners as was His 'passive' obedience. These two are inseparable. And although the terminology used to distinguish between them may not be altogether fortunate, yet the distinction is most valuable. By His obedience manifested in His passion, culminating in His death, Christ paid the penalty of sin, even eternal death. But He did much more for sinners. By His perfect obedience to the law of God throughout the whole of His earthly life He merited righteousness and life eternal. That positive phase of His work, too, was vicarious. 'Therefore as by the offence of one judgment came upon all men to condemnation; even so by the righteousness of one the free gift came upon all men unto justification of life. For as by one man's disobedience many were made sinners, so by the obedience of one shall many be made righteous' (Rom. 5 : 18, 19). Thus Christ by the atonement not only paid in full the debt of sinners; he also merited for them infinite riches.

The Gospel of Grace

The Bible has been named the book of salvation. In distinction from the book of general revelation, it is precisely that. Nature and history, valuable revelations of God though they are, say nothing about salvation from sin and spiritual death. The Bible, on the other hand, tells men all they need to know on that momentous subject.

What Scripture has to say concerning salvation is fully summed up in the term *salvation by grace*. And salvation by grace is nothing else than *salvation by God*. To the question how the sinner is to be saved, whether by his own efforts or by the grace of God, the gospel gives an unequivocal answer. It is no exaggeration to assert that the evangel teaches that salvation is a hundred per cent of the Triune God.

This is not to say that the sinner has no responsibility in the matter of his salvation. He must believe in Christ, and God holds him accountable for unbelief. Yet, saving faith is a gift of God. Nor may it be denied that in the process of his salvation the believer is in duty bound to become active. He is enjoined to work out his own salvation with fear and trembling. But when he obeys that command, he does so because it is God who not only once worked in him, but also keeps working in him, both to will and to do of his good pleasure (Phil. 2:12, 13).

God the Father saves.

From the foundation of the world He chose in Christ all those who will eventually inherit eternal life (Eph. 1:4). He chose them, not because of any foreseen good in them, but in His sovereign love (Eph. 1:5; Rom. 8:29). He gave them to the Son (John 17:6). Their salvation is assured, for no man can pluck them out of the Son's hand, and the Father, who gave them to Him, is greater than all, and no man is able to pluck them out of the Father's hand (John 10:28, 29). Those whom He loved from eternity God predestinated unto salvation. 'Moreover, whom he did predestinate, them he also called; and whom he called, them he also justified; and whom he justified, them he also glorified' (Rom. 8:30).

God the Son saves.

He merited salvation, the whole of it, both its negative and its positive aspects. He paid the debt of sinners to the last farthing. On the cross He was crushed by the curse of God which was due to them. In the stead of hell-deserving criminals He was forsaken of God. But also by His perfect obedience to the Father He merited for sinners righteousness, everlasting life and glory. In consequence, nothing remains for them to merit. It behoves each of them to say: 'Nothing in my hand I bring.'

Not only did the Son of God *merit* salvation; He also *bestows* salvation. That blessed truth is sometimes neglected. It is said that Christ by His saving work did no more than make salvation possible for all and that whether a given individual will actually be saved depends on the exercise by him of his free will. That is a most serious error. It amounts to saying that Christ's saving work does not save. It denies the power of the atonement. It robs Christ of His honour as Saviour. By making man his own saviour it spurns salvation by grace. The truth of the matter is that the atoning work of Christ saves all whom it was designed to save; namely, all whom the Father had given Him (John 17:9), His people (Matt. 1:21), His sheep (John 10:11), His church (Acts 20:28), God's elect (Rom. 8:32, 33).

God the Holy Spirit saves.

He applies salvation to sinners. He gives them hearts of flesh for hearts of stone (Ezek. 11:19). They are born again, their second birth being of the Spirit (John 3:5, 6). In consequence, they lay hold by faith on the Christ and all His saving benefits. Saving faith is a fruit of regeneration.

Faith is an act of man. That truth must be emphasized. To suppose that God does the believing for the sinner is an absurdity. What needs to be stressed no less is that faith is first of all a gift of God the Holy Spirit. Having identified coming to Him with believing on Him in the parallel statements: 'He that cometh to me shall never hunger; and he that believeth on me shall never thirst' (John 6:35), Jesus went on to say: 'No man can come to me, except the Father which hath sent me draw him' (John 6:44). He draws by His Spirit. Scripture accounts for the conversion of Lydia by saying, not that she opened her heart, but that the Lord opened her heart so that she attended to the things spoken by Paul (Acts 16:14). 'By grace are ye saved, through faith', Paul told the believers at Ephesus; and he added: 'And that not of yourselves: it is the gift of God' (Eph. 2:8). Whether the antecedent of 'it' is *faith* or *salva-*

tion by grace through faith, in either case faith is said to be a divine bestowal. The same apostle wrote to the church at Philippi: 'Unto you it is given in the behalf of Christ, not only to believe on him, but also to suffer for his sake' (Phil. 1:29). Both faith in Christ and suffering for Christ he regarded as gifts of God. And how emphatic is the Pauline dictum, 'I give you to understand . . . that no man can say that Jesus is the Lord, but by the Holy Ghost' (I Cor. 12:3)!

Are the unsaved to be told that faith is a gift of God? Most assuredly! Wholly, of course, the truth of the matter must be told them. To hide this truth from them would be irresponsible. To permit them to entertain the thought that they can believe of their own volition apart from the regenerating grace of the Holy Spirit is worse than irresponsible. It amounts to encouraging them in the belief that they are masters of their own fate, captains of their own souls. However, that faith is a gift of God is not the only truth to be impressed upon the lost. This truth must be coupled with another. As so often in Christian theology, so here also there are complementary truths both of which deserve the strongest stress. The sinner needs to be told emphatically that he *must* believe and that, in case he does not believe, the wrath of God will abide on him.

A worse predicament than that in which the unsaved sinner finds himself cannot be imagined. He *must* believe in Christ. If he does not, he will be damned. Yet he *cannot* believe. Of that dire predicament he must become aware. If he is made aware by the Holy Spirit, he will look away from self for salvation and abandon himself unreservedly to the grace of God. That is precisely the act of saving faith.

A certain man had been a paralytic for thirty-eight years. Together with a multitude of other impotent folk he lay at the pool Bethesda. He despaired of recovery. Jesus spoke: 'Arise, take up thy bed, and walk.' The paralytic was commanded to do that thing which of all things he could not do, and let no one think that he was not aware of his complete inability. But he also knew that his one hope of getting well lay in his doing that very thing. Fully conscious of his plight, he forgot himself and fixed his eye on Jesus. That was faith. By faith he was made whole (John 5: 1–9).

As Moses lifted up the serpent in the wilderness, so the Son of man had to be lifted up on Calvary's cross in order that whosoever has been fatally bitten by that venomous serpent, the devil, and, utterly helpless, looks to Him for grace, might not perish but have eternal life (John 3: 14, 15).

Such is the gospel of the saving grace of the Triune God. It must be the message of evangelism. He who responds to it in faith will sing:

> 'Tis not that I did choose Thee,
> For, Lord, that could not be;
> This heart would still refuse Thee,
> Hadst Thou not chosen me.
> Thou from the sin that stained me
> Hast cleansed and set me free;
> Of old Thou hast ordained me,
> That I should live to Thee.
>
> 'Twas sovereign mercy called me
> And taught my opening mind;
> The world had else enthralled me,
> To heavenly glories blind.
> My heart owns none before Thee,
> For Thy rich grace I thirst;
> This knowing, if I love Thee,
> Thou must have loved me first.

The Gospel of the New Birth

It has been said that the central message of evangelism must be the command, addressed to the unsaved, that they be born again. As a matter of fact, the Bible contains no such command. The Lord's statement to Nicodemus, 'Ye must be born again' (John 3:7), was an indicative, not an imperative. Jesus spoke of the new birth as an indispensable experience, yet not as a duty to be performed. Also Paul's admonition to the church at Ephesus, 'Awake thou that sleepest, and arise from the dead' (Eph. 5:14) may not be construed as a command to the spiritually dead sinner to come to life. It is clear that the entire passage of which this exhortation is a part was addressed to believing saints. It was said of them and to them: 'Ye were sometimes darkness, but now are ye light in the Lord' (vs. 8). But these saints were living in evil surroundings. Worse than that, they were being influenced adversely by their environment. They needed to be told to 'have no fellowship with the unfruitful works of darkness' (vs. 11). They were slumbering Christians, so to speak. Therefore the apostle enjoined them to awake from their sleep and to arise from among their spiritually dead neighbours. That is the force of the fourteenth verse.

The reason why Scripture nowhere commands the unregenerate to bring themselves to life is obvious. They are spiritually dead, 'dead in trespasses and sins' (Eph. 2:1). Not only is it a divine prerogative to bring them to life, but, when God Almighty exercises that prerogative, they are completely passive. In fact, this is the one and only part of the process of salvation in which man is passive. At every succeeding step he becomes active. The resurrection of

Lazarus may illustrate the point at issue. Jesus bade dead Lazarus: 'Come forth' (John 11:43). He did not command him to restore himself to life. By the word of His power Christ did that for him. And then living Lazarus came forth from the tomb.

Is it needless, then, to inform the sinner that he must be born again? Evidently Jesus did not so judge. He told Nicodemus just that. And beyond all reasonable doubt, He did so in condemnation of the religious externalism which was rife among the Jews of that day. They were wont, for instance, to boast of having Abraham as their father (cf. Luke 3:8). Nicodemus and his generation had need of being told that for entrance into the kingdom of God nothing less would suffice than a radical renewal of the heart. Who will deny that the present generation needs the same reminder? So does every generation of men. Birth from believing parents, the sacred rite of baptism, membership in the visible church, respectable behaviour, humanitarianism, even preaching in Christ's name (Matt. 7:22, 23), valuable assets though they are, do not constitute one a citizen of the kingdom. Without that spiritual rebirth which God alone can effect, no one can so much as see the kingdom.

In order to avoid confusion, it is necessary to distinguish between regeneration and conversion. To be sure, the term *new birth* can be used in various senses. It may designate the whole of subjective salvation, conversion and lifelong sanctification included. Likely a Scriptural instance of that use is afforded by I Peter 1:21, where believers are described as 'being born again, not of corruptible seed, but of incorruptible, by the word of God'. Ordinarily, however, Christian theology employs the term to denote that momentary transition from spiritual death to spiritual life which initiates the process of salvation. The new birth or regeneration in that sense must be distinguished from conversion. In regeneration the sinner is passive; in conversion he becomes active. According to the words of Jesus, 'The wind bloweth where it listeth, and thou hearest the sound thereof, but canst not tell whence it cometh and whither it goeth: so is every one that is born of the Spirit' (John 3 : 8); regeneration occurs in the sub-conscious; but conversion is a conscious experience of man. Regeneration is effected immediately by the Holy Spirit; that is to say, it is not brought about through the instrumentality of the Word, although it is doubtful, to say the least, whether it ever occurs unless the Word is present or about to be present in order to nourish the new life; but conversion is wrought by God by means of the Word. In theological terminology, regeneration is effected *cum Verbo*, conversion *per Verbum*. And conversion is a consequence, a manifestation, of the new birth.

Mention must here be made of what is popularly known as 'the whosoever-will gospel'. The Christian evangel is correctly so called. Time and again Scripture says that whosoever believes in Christ will be saved, and it hardly needs to be said that the human will participates in the act of faith. The very last invitation in the Bible reads: 'Let him that is athirst come. And whosoever will, let him take the water of life freely' (Rev. 22 : 17). However, let not the bearer of the gospel forget that the world of unregenerate men is one of universal *won't*. To declare to such a world that whosoever will may lay hold on eternal life, and then to depend on men to respond, is as futile as to proclaim to the serried ranks of the dead in a cemetery that whosoever will may arise. Conceived and born as he is in sin (Ps. 51 : 5), the mind of the natural man is 'enmity against God, for it is not subject to the law of God, neither indeed can be' (Rom. 8 : 7). To him applies Jesus' stern denunciation of His enemies, 'Ye will not come to me, that ye might have life' (John 5 : 40). 'So then it is not of him that willeth, nor of him that runneth, but of God that showeth mercy' (Rom. 9 : 16). But God does show mercy. By the life-giving operation of His Spirit in the hearts of men He makes them willing. In consequence, here and there and everywhere there are those who by the grace of God will. That truth, and it alone, makes 'the whosoever-will gospel' meaningful.

What also needs to be said is that the proof of regeneration is not a life of sinless perfection but rather a deep conviction of sin which causes one to run to Calvary and to kneel at the pierced feet of the Crucified One with the cry, 'Wash me, Saviour, or I die'; that he who is born again faces a life-long struggle between the old man and the new, so graphically depicted by the holy apostle in his confession, 'The good that I would I do not; but the evil that I would not, that I do' (Rom. 7 : 19); that nevertheless he will delight in the law of God after the inward man (Rom. 7 : 22); that the Holy Spirit will bear witness with his spirit that he is a child of God (Rom. 8 : 16); and that the indwelling Spirit of God with which he is sealed is the earnest of his heavenly inheritance (Eph. 1 : 13, 14), so that he may rest fully assured that He who has begun a good work in him will perform it until the day of Jesus Christ (Phil. 1 : 6).

The Gospel of the Kingdom

In foregoing chapters reference was made repeatedly to the evangel as the gospel of the kingdom. The kingdom concerned is variously denominated the kingdom of God, the kingdom of Christ, or the kingdom of heaven, and it has many aspects.

The Lord Jesus preached that gospel in His seven or eight parables of the kingdom recorded in Matthew 13. In the Sermon on the Mount he proclaimed the law or charter of the kingdom (Matt. 5, 6, 7). The eight beatitudes, with which that sermon begins, describe so many characteristics of every citizen of that kingdom (Matt. 5:3–12). And the Apostle Paul listed the blessings of the kingdom in the words: 'The kingdom of God is not meat and drink; but righteousness, and peace, and joy in the Holy Ghost' (Rom. 14:17).

It is of the greatest moment that Christ be preached, not only as Saviour, but also as King. What was said on that subject need not be repeated. But one important question relevant to the gospel of the kingdom must presently be faced.

For several decades now fundamentalists and modernists have been at odds as to whether the gospel is a message of individual or social salvation. Many a fundamentalist preacher, though aware that society is on fire, is interested only in rescuing individuals from the fire, not in putting the fire out. The modernist preacher, on the other hand, is intent on extinguishing the fire and thus hopes to benefit the individual, who, according to him, is largely the product of his environment. That difference is apparent also in present-day evangelism.

The fundamentalist is right so far as he goes, for that salvation is primarily a personal matter permits of no doubt. Yet he does not go far enough. He neglects the social teachings contained in the Word of God. For a few examples, Jesus had much to say on marriage and divorce (Matt. 5:27–32; Luke 16:18) and on the duty of the rich toward

[166]

the poor (Luke 16:19–25); and the apostle Paul, in addition to those subjects, dealt with the attitude of the Christian citizen to the civil magistrate (Rom. 13:1–7), the relation to each other of employers and employees (Eph. 6: 5–9; Col. 3:22—4:1), and slavery (Philemon). In evangelism the heart of the gospel must, of course, be foremost, but its social implications may not be ignored.

The fault of the social gospel of modernism is not that it would remedy social ills, but that it would accomplish this in a way which stands diametrically opposed to Christianity. Brushing aside the obvious truth that society can never be better than are the individuals which constitute it, it would improve the individual by improving society. It would rescue men from sin's consequences such as poverty and disease, rather than have them redeemed from sin itself by the blood of Christ. It would save the individual by what is termed the regeneration of society, not by the new birth supernaturally wrought by the Holy Spirit. It would by human effort get men out of the slums instead of getting the slums out of men by the grace of God. It neglects the profound truth so well expressed by that great evangelistic preacher, Charles Haddon Spurgeon, 'Take a thief to heaven, and the first thing he will do is to pick the pockets of the angels.'

There is another way of stating the difference between the individual gospel of fundamentalism and the social gospel of modernism.

Christ is both Saviour of men and Lord over all things. His lordship presupposes His saviourhood. *Because* He became obedient unto the death of the cross God put all things under His feet and gave Him to be 'the head over all things to the church' (Eph. 1:22).

By way of illustration, the evangel may be pictured as a

cone, the lower half of which represents the substitutionary atonement, the upper half the universal kingship of Christ.

Many a fundamentalist emphasizes the lower half, but neglects the upper. He proclaims a gospel, a true gospel, the basic gospel, but, it must be admitted, a truncated gospel.

The modernist would extol the upper half of the cone, but he divorces it from the lower. Yet, the upper half stands or falls with the lower. Christ is not King if He does not save. That reduces the gospel of modernism to a castle in the air. It is what Paul described as 'a different gospel which is not another' (Gal. 1:6, 7 ASV).

In Christian evangelism the cross of Christ and His crown belong together. What God has put together let not the evangelist put asunder.

A Comprehensive Gospel

What is the gospel? It has many facets not one of which may be neglected in the message of evangelism.

It is *a story*, the story of Jesus and His love, the story of the virgin birth of the Son of God, His holy life culminating in His atoning death, on which God the Father placed the stamp of approval by raising Him from the dead, His ascension into heaven and session at the right hand of God, the outpouring by Him of the Holy Spirit upon His church. That story excels in supernaturalism, for which reason theological liberalism rejects it and the so-called new orthodoxy would either demythologize it or place it in a category other than that of actual history. But the Bible relates it as plain history.

It is *a doctrine*, God's interpretation of that story, particularly the doctrine of Christ's divine person and that of

His vicarious atoning work. Modern unbelief will have nothing of it, but it is the wisdom of God.

It is *an invitation*, God's sincere offer of salvation to all to whom the gospel comes. And let it be well understood, that invitation is unconditional. God does not merely say to the sinner: 'I will give you eternal life if you repent and believe.' To be sure, He says that. But He also declares: 'I am earnestly inviting you to repent and believe in order that you may have life.' For God is 'not willing that any should perish, but that all should come to repentance' (II Peter 3:9).

It is *a promise*, God's promise of life everlasting to all who trust for salvation in the divine Christ and His redeeming work. Says God: 'Believe on the Lord Jesus Christ, and thou shalt be saved' (Acts 16:31).

It is *an appeal*, God's urgent and loving appeal to sinners to accept His offer and to comply with His invitation. God pleads with them: 'Turn ye, turn ye from your evil ways; for why will ye die?' (Ezek. 33:11). God beseeches them and Christ prays them to be reconciled to God (II Cor. 5:20).

It is *a demand*, God's demand that men believe on Christ. Here law and gospel merge. Gospel becomes law. When the Jews asked Jesus: 'What shall we do, that we might work the works of God?' He replied: 'This is the work of God, that ye believe on him whom he hath sent' (John 6:28, 29).

It is *a command*, God's command that those who trust in Christ as Saviour also gratefully serve Him as King of their lives. This is not an appendix to the evangel, but an integral part of it. In the Great Commission Christ instructed His disciples to teach men to observe all things whatsoever He had commanded. Believing in Christ and obeying Him are not two acts, but two phases of one act. Trusting Christ as Saviour and acknowledging Him as Lord are inseparable. The latter is the acid test of the former. That should be made clear to the sinner before he makes a decision in response to the gospel. 'A certain man said, Lord, I will follow thee whithersoever thou goest. And Jesus said unto him, Foxes have holes and birds of the air have nests; but the Son of man hath not where to lay his head. And he said unto another, Follow me. But he said, Lord, suffer me first to go and bury my father. Jesus said unto him, Let the dead bury their dead; but go thou and preach the kingdom of God. And another also said, Lord, I will follow thee; but let me first go bid them farewell which are at home at my house. And Jesus said unto him, No man, having put his hand to the plough, and looking back, is fit for the kingdom of God' (Luke 9:57–62). Before laying claim to discipleship, let everyone examine himself whether he is willing to meet the demands of discipleship, remembering the words of the Lord Jesus: 'Whosoever he be of you that forsaketh not all that he hath, he cannot be my disciple' (Luke 14:33).

An Exclusive Gospel

Admittedly, there are elements of truth in religions other than Christianity. Nevertheless, it must be insisted that Christianity is the only true religion and that all other religions are false.

The God of Christianity alone is God. Although He has revealed Himself more fully in the New Testament than in the Old, the God of both is identical. The first and foremost commandment of His law reads: 'Thou shalt have no other gods before me' (Exod. 20:3; Deut. 5:7). The great commandment of His entire law is: 'Thou shalt love the Lord thy God with all thy heart, and with all thy soul, and with all thy mind' (Deut. 6:5; Matt. 22:37). He is a jealous God who will brook no other. The Psalmist exclaimed: 'Thou art God alone' (Ps. 86:10). To the believers in idolatrous Corinth the apostle wrote: 'Though there be that are called gods, whether in heaven or in earth (as there be gods many and lords many), but to us there is but one God, the Father, of whom are all things, and we in him' (I Cor. 8:5, 6). Man worships either the Creator or the creature (Rom. 1:25). The Creator alone is God. All other gods are idols.

The one true God has revealed Himself supernaturally and infallibly in the inscripturated Word, known as the Bible, and in the personal Word, His Son. Such 'sacred' books as the Zend-Avesta of Zoroastrianism, the Vedas of Brahmanism, the Tripitaka of Buddhism, the Koran of Mohammedanism, are not to be compared with the Bible. And Buddha, Confucius, Mohammed, and all human founders of the religions of mankind were but fallible and sinful mortals, not to be named in the same breath with the Son of God.

Jesus Christ is the one and only Saviour. He Himself declared majestically: 'I am the way, the truth, and the life; no man cometh unto the Father but by me' (John 14:6). Peter, filled with the Holy Spirit, told the Jewish Sanhedrin: 'Neither is there salvation in any other; for there is none other name under heaven given among men, whereby we must be saved' (Acts 4:12). Because He is a perfect Saviour, there is need of no other. 'He is able also to save them to the uttermost that come unto God by him, seeing he ever liveth to make intercession for them' (Heb. 7:25). All other saviours are pretenders.

The Christian way of salvation is the one and only way. All other religions teach salvation by human effort; Christianity alone teaches salvation by the grace of God. All other religions say: 'Do and live.' Christianity says: 'Live and do.' It follows that Pelagianism, both ancient and modern, is pagan. Pagan is William E. Henley's boast:

> It matters not how strait the gate,
> How charged with punishments the scroll.
> I am the master of my fate;
> I am the captain of my soul.

Christian is Christina G. Rossetti's cry:

> None other Lamb, none other Name,
> None other Hope in heaven or earth or sea,
> None other Hiding-place from guilt and shame,
> None beside Thee.

Sad to say, not every Christian theology has held with complete and unswerving consistency to the Scriptural teaching of salvation by the grace of the Triune God. It may be said without hesitation that the Reformed theology excels in consistency at this vital point of Christian doctrine. Its glory is that it ascribes all the glory for the sinner's salvation to God.

Yet that is not the entire picture. Confused though his thinking may be – and all human thinking suffers from imperfection – in his heart of hearts every Christian trusts for salvation in God alone. *The Westminster Shorter Catechism* defines faith in Jesus Christ as 'a saving grace, whereby we receive and rest upon Him *alone* for salvation, as He is offered to us in the gospel' (Answer 86). That is the essence of saving faith. Every Christian has it. And breathes there a child of God who, when confronting the question whether he owes his being a believer to himself or to the grace of God, will not in grateful humility give all the credit and all the praise to the Holy Spirit?

An Offensive Gospel

While the whole of the Christian gospel displeases the natural man, especially two of its aspects make it offensive.

One of these aspects is its uncompromising teaching of salvation by the grace of God and by that grace alone. Nothing could be more humiliating for man. He is utterly undeserving of salvation, and he is utterly unable to save himself. He deserves only eternal hell and if he had to contribute but one stitch of his own making to his celestial garment, he would be eternally lost. His very believing is 'the gift of God', and his good works were 'afore prepared' by God (Eph. 2:8, 10 ASV).

The other aspect of the Christian evangel which offends, and even infuriates, the natural man is its claim to exclusiveness. He denounces that claim as intolerant and bigoted.

Yet that offensive gospel must be proclaimed without the slightest compromise, for compromise is adulteration. The truth must be spoken, the whole truth, albeit always compassionately, patiently, and in love. For the Christ of that gospel, although a stumblingblock to the Jews and foolishness to the Greeks, is to them that are called, both Jews and Greeks, 'the power of God and the wisdom of God' (I Cor. 1:23, 24).

14: God and Zeal for Evangelism

Zeal in Another Age

The sixteenth-century Reformers and the churches of the Reformation have often been charged with almost complete indifference to evangelism. Strange to say, that charge has been levelled against them, not only by Roman Catholic but also by Protestant writers. Granted that Protestant enthusiasm for missions reached greater heights in the nineteenth and twentieth centuries, those who make the aforementioned accusation overlook several facts.

The Reformers were engaged in a strenuous campaign aiming at the evangelization of Europe. Theirs was a programme of most intensive home missions. And, let it be said emphatically, home missions are not a whit less worthy than are foreign missions. The Bible was translated into the vernacular, the language of the common people. Whereas in the Roman church ritual had crowded out the gospel, Protestantism stressed preaching as the church's chief task. Men from every part of the Continent, as well as the British Isles, sat at the feet of Calvin and were taught by him to proclaim the Word of God. Besides, the Genevan Reformer carried on a truly cosmopolitan correspondence in the interest of the evangel. To someone in England he wrote: 'God has created the entire world that it should be the theatre of His glory by the spread of His gospel.'

As regards foreign missions, the churches of the Reformation suffered from two serious handicaps. They were involved in a hard struggle for their very existence, and many of the newly discovered lands in Asia, Africa, and America were under the control of such Roman Catholic nations as Spain and Portugal, which were intolerant of Protestantism.

In view of those hindrances, it is truly amazing how active was Protestantism in the evangelization of foreign lands. As early as 1555 Calvin and the French Huguenot Admiral Coligny organized a mission to Brazil. Calvin himself secured four missionaries for that project, to which number eight were added by Calvinists residing outside of Geneva. Due to Roman Catholic persecution, five of those missionaries were murdered and the rest were repatriated to Europe. In 1559 Gustav Wasa of Sweden brought the gospel to Lapland. In 1577 Wenceslaus Budovatz, a Hungarian Calvinist, began missions in Mohammedan Turkey. He wrote a defence of the Christian religion for Moslems. The Synod of Dort, which drew up the so-called five points of Calvinism, concerned itself seriously with foreign missions. That was in 1618 and 1619. In 1622 there was established in Leyden a Reformed seminary for the training of missionaries. While engaged in its war of independence from Spain, Dutch Protestantism sent missionaries to the East Indies and Ceylon. At the urging of English and Scottish pastors, Parliament passed an ordinance creating 'The Corporation for the Propagation of the Gospel in New England'. In 1646 it appointed John Eliot as its first missionary, and he established seventeen mission posts among North American Indians. About the middle of the seventeenth century there appeared two Dutch works on missions, both of which continue worthy of attention to the present day. They are *De Conversione Indorum* by Johannes Hoornbeek and *De Plantatione Ecclesiarum* by

Gijsbertus Voetius. The Danish Halle Mission entered India in 1706. Lutheran Thomas V. Weston began his labours in Lapland in 1727.

The foregoing record, incomplete as it is, gives conclusive evidence that the Protestant churches of Europe were actively engaged in foreign missions long before William Carey, often referred to as the founder of modern missions, sailed for India in 1793.

In view of these facts, it is difficult to account for the accusation that the churches of the Reformation gave little, if indeed any, evidence of interest in evangelism. A possible explanation may be an unsympathetic attitude on the part of the accusers to the theology of the Reformation. That such a Roman Catholic author as Joseph Schmidlin would be prejudiced against that theology might be expected, but even so highly respected a Protestant writer as Julius Richter is not altogether without fault on that score. That the Reformation was an intensely doctrinal movement, as is evinced by Luther's Ninety-five Theses and Calvin's *Institutes of the Christian Religion*, is not appreciated, by and large, as it should be. And that the doctrine of predestination, to which Luther subscribed as well as Calvin, can only prove a damper on evangelistic zeal is a widespread misapprehension. As a matter of fact, in the *Institutes* and his commentaries, as well as his sermons, Calvin manifested a deep concern for the spread of the gospel to 'all states and all peoples'. Commenting on the Great Commission, he said: 'The Lord commands the ministers of the gospel to go to a distance, in order to spread the doctrine of salvation in every part of the world.' It has been said truly that the Reformation was nothing else than a rediscovery of Paul. It rediscovered that apostle as a teacher of sovereign divine election, but also as God's chosen vessel to bear His name before the gentiles (Acts 9: 15).

Zeal without Knowledge

More than one historian has contrasted periods in which the Christian church was engaged in doctrinal controversy with periods in which it was devoted to the spread of the gospel. As a general rule, those who play up that contrast reprove the church for the former periods and laud it for the latter.

A similar attitude is prevalent among Protestants today. Practically all are, or at least claim to be, zealous for evangelism. Very few, on the other hand, take an interest in Christian doctrine. In fact, the view is widely held and boldly advocated that it is high time for Protestantism, which was in the past split into many denominations on the rock of doctrinal divergency, to sink those differences. What is insisted upon most strenuously is that Protestant missionaries ought not to trouble with such differences those among whom they labour, but should present a united front. The modern ecumenical movement, which is characterized by a lowest common denominator theology, originated in the mission fields of the world.

Granted that it would be most unwise to ask African pagans to take sides on every doctrinal issue that has ever divided Protestants and that it would be irresponsible to reproduce on that continent every Protestant denomination existing, let us say, in North America, the aforenamed attitude is deserving of vigorous condemnation.

When is Protestantism going to outgrow the trite and misleading, no, utterly false, slogan that Christianity is not a doctrine but a life? Of course, Christianity is a life, but it also most certainly is a doctrine. To use an old, and ad-

[177]

mittedly inadequate, illustration, orthodoxy is to Christianity what the bones are to the human body. Bones alone do not constitute a body. Isolated from the rest of the body, they are a skeleton. So orthodoxy without life or, in the words of James, 'faith without works', is dead (James 2: 26). But bones, too, are essential to the human body. A body without bones simply is not a body. Neither is Christianity without doctrine Christianity. And let no one think that the bones of a living body are dead. They share in the life of the entire body. So Christian doctrine, too, is vital. To change the simile and to go far beyond it, truth is the very heart of Christianity.

It is rather generally agreed that the evangelist is to convey the Word of God. But just what does that mean? Does it signify, as both modernism and the so-called new orthodoxy say, that he must preach Christ, the personal Word, to whom a fallible and faulty Bible witnesses? Or must the position of the historic Christian church be maintained that he is to proclaim the infallible and inerrant inscripturated Word of God as well as the personal Word of the written Word?

By common consent, the evangelist is to preach Christ. But which Christ? Obviously, the answer to that question is a matter of doctrine. Is it to be the Christ of modernism —a Christ who did not exist from eternity as the second person of the Trinity, whose picture as painted in the four gospels is largely mythological, who was not born of a virgin and whose body has long since returned to dust, and who either was divine only in the sense in which all men are divine and therefore should not be worshipped or, at best, was a man who became God? Or is it to be the Christ of the Bible, about whose person and natures the early church debated for centuries until finally, in the year 451,

[178]

the Council of Chalcedon, speaking for the Christian church as a whole, concluded that He is 'perfect in Godhead and also perfect in manhood', that He is 'one person . . . the Son, and only begotten, God the Word', and that His two natures, divine and human, exist 'unconfusedly, unchangeably, indivisibly, and inseparably'?

Again by common consent, the evangelist must proclaim salvation. But salvation how – by the sinner's own efforts or by the grace of God? Christendom confronted that issue early in the fifth century. It was debated strenuously by Augustine, bishop of Hippo, in Africa, and the British monk Pelagius. Augustine's position was Biblical, hence Christian; and the church adopted it.

But the church found it difficult to uphold that position with consistency. The heresy of the meritoriousness of good works came to pervade Christendom. That the sinner is saved by human merits in addition to the merits of Christ became the official teaching of the church. This doctrinal error was challenged by the Reformation. Protestantism insisted that the merits of Christ constitute the sole ground of salvation. And that truth is of the very essence of the evangel.

How clear that the historic church was by no means wasting its time and energy when it engaged in doctrinal controversy! Rather, under the guidance of the Spirit of truth (John 16:13) it was upholding the gospel. Had it failed to defend the gospel against the corruption of heresy, the church of today would have no evangel to proclaim. Today's church, too, has no more solemn duty than to maintain purity of doctrine. The performance of that obligation need not interfere with evangelism but, contrariwise, is in its interest and essential to it. With it Christian evangelism stands or falls.

A more zealous evangelist than the Apostle Paul never trod the earth. He, too, engaged in doctrinal controversy. And he did not do it in mealy-mouthed fashion. Militantly he declared: 'Though we, or an angel from heaven, preach any other gospel unto you than that which we have preached unto you, let him be accursed' (Gal. 1:8). He was zealous for sound doctrine *because* he was zealous for evangelism. His zeal for the one matched his zeal for the other. They were of one piece.

Zeal for evangelism divorced from interest in Christian doctrine is 'zeal not according to knowledge' (Rom. 10:2).

Such zeal manifests itself patently in neglect of the indoctrination of church members, notably of the children. Doctrinal preaching is unpopular today. Church members are willing to be told from the pulpit what to *do*, but hardly what to *believe*. Most of them have no interest in theology, and of the few that do each wants to be his own doctor of theology. Their pastors willingly let them have their way. Time was when covenant children were instructed by their pastors in the truths of the Christian religion. Today few attempt that. A missionary on furlough from Arabia once chided an audience of Americans, all of them presumably mission-minded, for doing less for the religious education of their own children than they were doing for the religious education of Moslem youth. The church which neglects the indoctrination of the rising generation will soon have no missionaries to send out, certainly no missionaries who are zealous to declare the only true evangel.

Zeal Oriented to Theology

The charge that theological concern is incompatible with evangelistic zeal has perhaps been laid most frequently at the door of adherents of the Reformed theology. Granted that not everyone who professes the Reformed faith is zealous for missions, granted also that Moravianism, Pietism, and Methodism have provided powerful stimuli for Protestant missions, it can easily be shown that the Reformed faith, properly conceived and heartily believed, is definitely conducive to evangelistic zeal. A reminder of some previously discussed facets of that faith will make this clear.

Divine sovereignty is the fundamental principle of Calvinism. It may safely be asserted that the Calvinist stresses the sovereignty of God more than other Christians are wont to do. Now His sovereignty comes to prominent expression in three aspects of the one will of God: His secret or decretive will, His revealed or preceptive will, and what may be termed the will of His desire. From whatever angle one views the sovereign will of God, its consideration can only engender a zeal for the spread of the gospel.

From eternity God elected certain persons in Christ to eternal life (Eph. 1:4). Let no one confuse that truth with theological fatalism or philosophical determinism. God chose in love. And God does not by main force take the elect to heaven. He ordained that they would be saved by the gospel, and by no other means. It follows that election demands evangelism. It also follows that election guarantees results for evangelism. If it were left to sinners, totally depraved as they are, to respond of their own volition to the gospel in faith, not one would respond. As it is, the God who chose them is certain to endow the elect with grace to believe. All that was said in an earlier chapter, but it may here be repeated with added emphasis.

The Great Commission is a command of the sovereign God. Obviously, the more seriously one takes the divine sovereignty, so much the more will one feel oneself in holy duty bound to carry out that command. The Calvinist, of all Christians, will say: 'Necessity is laid upon me; yea, woe is unto me, if I preach not the gospel' (I Cor. 9:16). A sovereign command of God which comes to everyone who hears the gospel is the command to believe in Christ. The truth that no one can believe unless God draws him by the irresistible grace of the Holy Spirit (John 6:44) does not detract an iota from the binding force of that command. Nor is there anything unreasonable about that command. For God to require of man to do something which he could not do as he came forth from the hands of the Creator, as, for instance, to alter the orbit of the earth around the sun, would indeed be unreasonable, and unjust, too. But when God requires of man that he put his trust in God, He demands only what man was able to do originally. Although man in his fallen state no longer has that ability, he alone is to blame for its loss. God's right is not affected. So the sinner *must* believe, or he will perish everlastingly. What an incentive for issuing that command to the lost!

The Reformed Christian does not shun Biblical paradoxes. To be sure, he will have no part of the irrationalism of neo-orthodoxy. The teaching that truth is self-contradictory he rejects with all his might. But if he finds taught unmistakably in Scripture two truths which he cannot possibly reconcile with each other at the bar of human reason, he gladly subjects his logic to the divine Word. A most striking Biblical paradox is that God, who sovereignly chose out of the fallen race of men a fixed number to everlasting life, yet offers to all men without distinction eternal life and, when doing so, assures them that nothing would please Him more than their acceptance of His offer. God assures sinners everywhere that He 'will have all men to be saved' (I Tim. 2:4). That, too, is an expression of the sovereignty of God, and its proclamation is a recognition of that sovereignty. The Calvinist declares it passionately.

Practically everybody knows that the apostle Paul was the greatest missionary the Christian church has ever had. Though admittedly 'the least of the apostles, and not meet to be called an apostle', he could testify: 'By the grace of God I am what I am; and his grace which was bestowed on me was not in vain; but I laboured more abundantly than they all' (I Cor. 15:9, 10). What everyone also knows who has read the letters of the same apostle thoughtfully is that he was wont to stress the sovereignty of God most vehemently. That the church's foremost teacher of divine sovereignty was at once the church's foremost missionary, was no accident. By all the rules of sound logic that had to be. Consistency demanded it.

Another distinctively Reformed teaching is that of the covenant of grace. Like the doctrine of election, it, too, is often said to be inimical to missionary zeal. However, if properly understood, it, no less than the doctrine of election, is certain to engender zeal for evangelism. The covenant of grace does indeed spell particularism and separation, but not as ends in themselves, rather as means to the end of universalism. God commanded Abraham to get himself out of his country and from his kindred and from his father's house in order that in him all families of the earth might be blessed (Gen. 12:1–3). So broad a concept is the covenant of grace that the covenant of grace may be said to be wherever the gospel is proclaimed. And as the covenant God in the bestowal of saving grace is wont to take family ties into account, the evangelist may rest assured that not only will his labours not be in vain in the Lord (I Cor. 15:58) for the present, but they will continue

[183]

to bear fruit from generation to generation. That, too, was said previously but can bear emphatic repetition.

The Reformed faith provides the strongest and noblest motive for evangelism. Love for unworthy self and love for unlovely man are indeed worthy motives, but neither of these is the ultimate motive. The ultimate, hence the most compelling, motive must be love for the altogether adorable God.

The Reformed faith presents the purest and most comprehensive message of evangelism. It emphasizes with unswerving consistency the Scriptural teaching of salvation by the grace of God. On that most significant score it is at complete odds with modernism, but it also surpasses Lutheranism, with its synergistic conception of salvation, and Arminianism, which makes God dependent on man in the personal appropriation of salvation. And it embraces 'the whole counsel of God' (Acts 20:27 ASV), the seemingly contradictory, yet to the mind of God perfectly harmonious, teachings of particular divine election and universal divine love included.

The Reformed faith proposes the highest aim for evangelism. It is not the salvation of souls. Nor is it the growth of Christ's church. Nor yet is it the coming of Christ's kingdom. All those aims of evangelism are important, even of inestimable importance. Yet they are but means to the accomplishment of that end for which all things were brought into being and continue to exist, unto which God does all that He does, in which the whole of history will one day culminate, and on which the never-ending ages of eternity will be focused—*the glory of God*.

In short, the Reformed Christian, of all Christians, ought to be most zealous for evangelism. If he is truly – not just nominally – Reformed, he will be.

[184]

15: God and the Method of Evangelism

GENERALLY SPEAKING, THE METHOD OF EVAN-gelism must be determined by the principles of evangelism. On that proposition there is hardly room for difference of opinion. However, it may not be inferred that a principle is involved in every detail of method. Not infrequently a course of action is properly determined by expediency. In other words, there are *adiaphora* here, matters which have divine approval without being divinely commanded.

To deny that, is to overlook the self-evident fact that conditions and circumstances vary greatly in different places. Nor is it good theology. God is a God of law and order, to be sure, but He is also a God of infinite variety. No two leaves on all the trees in the world has He made to be of exactly the same size and shape. And, while there is but one way of salvation, namely Christ, no two persons walking that way have completely identical experiences. Variety has its place also in evangelistic method.

This chapter will deal with evangelistic method only in so far as it is closely related to evangelistic principles. In other words, the methods to be considered have theological relevance.

The Precedence of the Organized Church

The Christian church is the God-ordained agent of evangelism. That truth applies primarily to the church as an organization. To the apostles, the nucleus of the organized New Testament church, Christ gave the commission to make disciples of all the nations (Matt. 28:19). At Pentecost the organized church was empowered by the Holy Spirit to perform that task (Acts 2). It was the organized church at Antioch in Syria which, under the guidance of the Spirit, sent forth Barnabas and Saul as missionaries (Acts 13:1–4).

It does not follow that individual believers may not witness to the gospel. They certainly must. Nor does it follow that groups of individual Christians, representing the church as an organism rather than an organization, may not engage in evangelistic effort. They may, and it can even be said that under certain circumstances they must. Yet, the fact that according to Scripture the organized church is the primary agent of evangelism has some definite implications as to method. Four of them follow.

In the first place, the organized church *must* conduct evangelism. Evangelistic activity is a mark of the true church. Therefore the organized church may not leave the performance of that task to its individual members nor to voluntary associations of its members.

Secondly, voluntary associations of believers may not, under normal circumstances, presume to displace the organized church as the agent of evangelism. At most, they are to supplement the work of the church. Mission boards and evangelistic committees independent of ecclesiastical control are in order only when the organized church fails to perform its God-assigned duty and all efforts to persuade it to do its duty have failed.

Thirdly, church councils such as the National Council of the Churches of Christ and the International Council of Christian Churches, to name two of several, are not churches. A council of churches is not itself a church, nor should it be permitted to become a super-church. For that reason such organizations ought to refrain from usurping functions which properly belong to the constituent churches. Prominent among those functions is evangelism.

Fourthly, one reason, no doubt, why God has assigned the work of evangelism primarily to the organized church is that He would have converts unite with the church. The aim of evangelism is not merely the salvation of individual souls, but the addition of saved souls to the church. Generally speaking, it is more likely that evangelism conducted by the organized church will contribute to the growth of the church than that evangelism conducted by voluntary associations of believers will lead to that result.

The Priority of Educational Evangelism

Two methods of evangelism are often contrasted with each other: mass evangelism and personal evangelism. It is not necessary to advocate one of these to the exclusion of the other. They may well complement one another. What must needs be pointed out is that, whichever of these methods is employed, in either case teaching, instructing, educating, must have priority.

On the necessity of personal evangelism there is full agreement; not on the propriety in this day and age of mass evangelism. As a matter of fact, there are valid arguments against mass evangelism as popularly conceived and usually conducted today.

Historically the appeal of mass evangelism has been largely to the will and the emotions. That holds of the evangelistic preaching of both Wesley and Whitefield, to a limited extent to that of Jonathan Edwards, and most certainly to that of Dwight L. Moody, Charles G. Finney,

Billy Sunday, and the Gipsy Smiths of more recent times. There was some justification for the nature of that appeal. All the aforenamed evangelists had good reason to assume on the part of their audiences a measure of knowledge of the basic teachings of Christianity. Today that assumption is no longer valid, not even in such supposedly Christian lands as England and the United States of America. The general populace is well-nigh abysmally ignorant of Bible history and Bible doctrine, as well as Bible ethics. In consequence, evangelistic preaching must today be first of all instructive. People need to be taught the Word of God. Here it may be recorded that Billy Graham's oft-repeated phrase, 'The Bible says', is evidence of his putting forth an effort – albeit a too feeble one – in that direction.

There is an additional reason why evangelism of the educational type should be emphasized today. However ignorant men may be, and actually are, of the Christian religion, it can hardly be denied that secular education so called, although seriously lacking in thoroughness, is much more widespread than it was only a few decades ago. The general level of intelligence has risen appreciably. That holds even of some pagan lands. In these United States almost everybody is getting a high school education, and our colleges are crowded to the doors and beyond. In consequence there is much dissatisfaction with predominantly volitional and emotional evangelism. There is a rising and just demand that the evangelist show the reasonableness of the Christian religion. That demand must be met by a Scriptural apologetic.

In the minds of many the traditional 'altar call' is part and parcel of mass evangelism. To it as frequently given there is a more serious objection than that of excessive voluntarism and emotionalism. Behind it often lurks a most faulty theology. It is assumed that unregenerate man has the ability of his own free volition to accept Christ in faith, and that it is the evangelist's task by a powerful and sustained appeal to the natural man's will and emotions to prevail upon him to exercise that ability; that is to say, in popular parlance, to 'make him come across'.

In the parable of the sower, more correctly denominated the parable of the soil, Jesus has called attention to a peril associated with traditional mass evangelism. Said the Lord: 'He that received the seed into stony places, the same is he that heareth the word, and anon with joy receiveth it; yet hath he not root in himself, but dureth for a while; for when tribulation or persecution ariseth because of the word, by and by he is offended' (Matt. 13:20, 21). Joy is an emotion. Sudden joy is apt to be strongly emotional. Evidently Jesus had in mind the person who is affected only emotionally by the gospel but has neither undergone a change of heart nor had his mind enlightened by the Word and the Spirit of God. Yet He cannot have meant that the Holy Spirit's gift of a new heart and His application of the Word to that heart will leave one emotionally cold. His first reaction will not be joy, but sorrow for sin, repentance toward God, a fleeing to the crucified Saviour. Joy will follow.

Is mass evangelism *as such* to be condemned? Not at all! There is a clear instance of it in the New Testament, and this instance met with unqualified divine approval. Peter's Pentecostal sermon was preached to thousands. Through it approximately three thousand were converted. But the fact may not be overlooked that Peter's audience consisted largely of dispersed Jews, who no doubt, were acquainted with the Old Testament Scriptures; and that, Peter's sermon, while addressed to the whole man, to all the functions of man's soul, as all preaching should be, was, so far as recorded, primarily instructive. The apostle proved from the prophets that crucified, resurrected, and ascended Jesus of Nazareth was in very deed the Messiah, and he informed his hearers that it was that Jesus who on this day had poured out the Spirit (Acts 2:14-40).

Mass evangelism is to be encouraged for the obvious reason that the gospel must be brought as soon as is possible to as many as can be reached. The evangelist who faces a massive audience should be grateful for his opportunity. But his message must by all means be of the right kind. While it should appeal to men's intellects, wills, emotions, and imaginations, men must first of all be taught the Word of God. It can hardly be said too often that according to the Great Commission evangelism is primarily teaching. In any day, particularly in this day, there is a crying need for educational evangelism.

Mass evangelism should pave the way for personal evangelism. When preaching to large crowds, the evangelist must give opportunity in one way or another to those who would learn more of the way of salvation to so indicate. And it is a matter of supreme importance that those who express that desire be further instructed.

Thus personal evangelism ought to result from mass evangelism. Yet, personal evangelism is not dependent on mass evangelism. It has strong claims of its own. In the Bible it occupies a place of exceeding prominence. The story of God's own dealing with Cain (Gen. 4:9-15), of Nathan's rebuke administered to backslidden David (II Sam. 12:1-14), of the Lord's preaching to Nicodemus (John 3), of the conversion of the Samaritan woman (John 4:1-29), the Ethiopian eunuch (Acts 8:26-39), the Roman centurion Cornelius (Acts 10), the Philippian jailer (Acts

16:25-34), and the slave Onesimus (Philemon) are but a few of numerous instances. The reason is apparent. Conversion is an intensely personal experience. Nothing can be more personal. And let it be noted that personal evangelism ordinarily affords a better opportunity for thorough and effective teaching than does mass evangelism.

Every church should have a class, preferably conducted by the pastor, for the instruction of inquirers after the way of salvation. And if at times there be but one seeking soul to be dealt with, this work must still go on. 'Joy shall be in heaven over one sinner that repenteth' (Luke 15:7).

The Comprehensive Method

What is the comprehensive method of evangelism? Briefly put, its advocates would not merely have the evangelist convey the gospel of salvation from sin and death, but also have him impart the benefits of culture. Among such benefits such matters as sanitation, medical care, hospitals, schools, adequate housing, effective methods of agriculture, an abundance of wholesome food, and decency in human relations rate high. Recently, planned parenthood has been added to the list.

Now culture needs to be defined. Much that is unworthy of the name is often subsumed under it. To say the very least, some motives and methods of birth control cannot pass the test of Christian ethics, and whatsoever goes contrary to true religion is also at variance with true culture. Yet, properly conceived, culture is a blessing. In the beginning God gave man a mandate to subdue the earth (Gen. 1:28). Man's efforts to carry out that mandate have under the guidance of the common grace of God resulted in numerous blessings to the human race.

Much can be said for the comprehensive method of evangelism. As was pointed out under the head *God and the Approach of Evangelism*, Jesus employed that method in principle when by His miracles of healing He prepared men psychologically for the reception of the evangel. He commanded His disciples to use the same method when He instructed them, not only to preach the gospel, but also to heal the sick (Luke 9:2). Furthermore, it is an undeniable fact that, although much culture was in evidence in such pagan lands, to name a few, as ancient Egypt, Babylon, Persia, Greece, and Rome, the fullest enjoyment of the blessings of culture comes in the wake of Christianity. Surely, it is altogether fitting, when introducing to the Christian religion the people of a backward pagan land or the dwellers in the slums of our own big cities, to let them share in such concomitant benefits of Christianity.

That there is a proper use of the comprehensive method having been gladly granted, a stern warning against its abuse is in order. It is not at all unusual for proponents of this method to pervert it. The benefits of culture are stressed to the neglect of the evangel. Briefly put, civilization is substituted for Christianization as the end of what purports to be evangelism.

It is far from superfluous to insist on what ought to be perfectly obvious – that evangelism must be evangelism. The one task of the evangelist is to bring the gospel. In doing so, he may make use of various helps. But whatever helps he may employ, they must remain subsidiary to the performance of his task. The spread of the gospel is his sole business. And the gospel is the good news of what God has done in Christ to save lost men from sin's guilt and power and pollution, to impart to them both righteousness and holiness, to qualify them for His service on earth, to effect

[192]

their escape from hell and their entrance into the perfect and eternal bliss of heaven.

Modern Means of Transportation and Communication

Trivial though it may seem, the reminder is in order that the world of today is in many respects quite different from the world of Paul, the missionary. For one thing, it is ever so much smaller. Relatively speaking, Tokio is much nearer to New York City than was Rome to Jerusalem in Paul's day. Modern means of transportation, most notably the jet plane, have brought that about. And such modern means of communication as radio have practically annihilated distance.

Not all Christians appreciate such inventions as they should. Some look askance at them. But that should not be. Whether consciously or unconsciously, modern man is working hard at his God-given mandate to subdue the earth (Gen. 1 : 28). And such inventions as the aforenamed represent the discovery by man of laws of nature laid down by God, as well as the discovery and harnessing by man of forces called into being at the beginning of time by the Creator.

While it is altogether possible, and even likely, that, after the manner of Mrs. Shelley's mythical Frankenstein, the human race will eventually go a long way toward destroying itself by its inventions, the truth may not be overlooked that God would have His church make diligent and efficient use of modern means of transportation and communication for the early spread of the gospel to the remotest corners of earth, thus hastening the day of Christ's triumphant coming (Matt. 24 : 14).

That, too, is a demand of sound theology.

The Indigenous Church

Indigenous means *native*.

In recent decades many have insisted that very soon after a church has come into being in a foreign land through the preaching of the gospel, the missionary in charge should proceed to another field and leave it to the newly organized native church to make shift for itself. One of the first and most ardent advocates of such procedure was John Livingston Nevius, who laboured as a Presbyterian missionary in China and Japan from 1854 until his death in 1893. The method developed by him, and sometimes named for him, was soon adopted by missionaries in Korea and there met with its most conspicuous success.

The Nevius or indigenous method of missions insists on four particulars: self-support, self-government, self-education, and self-propagation by the native church.

It is not at all difficult to adduce valid arguments for this method. The following are some of them.

As to self-support, as a rule it is not wholesome for a native church to remain financially dependent on a church or churches in a Christian land. Rather, a grace which all converts to Christianity must be taught is that of sacrificial giving. And, if a native church sustains itself, the funds from which the missionary who was instrumental in founding it draws his support become available for the further spread of the gospel.

As to self-government, appeal can justly be made to the fact that Paul and Barnabas, on their return to Antioch from their first missionary journey, visited the places where the seed sown by them had borne fruit and 'ordained them elders in every church' (Acts 14:23). A large measure of self-government was certainly involved. It may also be

[194]

argued, and correctly so, that every local or particular church, instead of being a small part of the mystical body of Christ, is a manifestation of that body in its entirety or, in theological language, an *ecclesia completa*. From that principle it follows that no church may lord it over another church.

As to self-education, every convert must be impressed with the fact that he has only a small beginning of the knowledge he ought to have and that, therefore, through diligent study of the Word of God in private and in collaboration with others, he must grow in grace and in the knowledge of Jesus Christ (II Peter 3:18). Also, the native pastor has no more urgent task than to teach his flock the Word of God.

As to self-propagation, each member of a native church needs to be told that he shares in the universal prophethood of believers, that it is his solemn duty to confess Christ before men (Matt. 10:32, 33) and to show forth the praises of Him who has called him out of darkness into His marvellous light (I Peter 2:9). If the membership of the native church is faithful in that regard, the missionary who helped found it will be in a position to follow the example of Paul, who, according to his own testimony, strove to preach the gospel where Christ was not yet named, lest he should build on another man's foundation (Rom. 15:20), and thus the spread of the gospel will be accelerated. In many instances, too, a native evangelist may be expected to be more influential with his as yet unsaved neighbours than a foreign missionary can be.

Certain current events on the world scene afford a strong argument for the indigenous method. Now that Christian missionaries from other lands are to all intents and purposes barred from Communist China, one may well wish that the native Christian communions in that land have learned the practice of self-support, self-government, self-education, and self-propagation. What has happened there may happen elsewhere.

The Scriptural teaching of the preservation or perseverance of the saints has been used to bolster the indigenous method. It is argued that, since it is certain that God, who began a good work in recent converts, will perform it until the day of Jesus Christ (Phil. 1:6), the missionary who was instrumental in bringing them to the faith can safely depart at any time. Now the doctrine of the eternal security of believers is certainly a most precious one. Yet the aforenamed argumentation must be judged to be too simple. It leaves largely out of account the truth that salvation is not merely a momentary experience but a lifelong process. And it fails to do justice to the plain fact that, in causing His children to persevere in the faith and to grow in holiness, God employs His Word as a means. Did not Jesus intercede for His disciples: 'Sanctify them through thy truth' (John 17:17)? It follows that it may well be to the spiritual advantage of the members of a newly organized native church that the missionary continue for a good while to teach them the Word of God.

Although in the main a good case can be made for the method under discussion, the principle of the indigenous church, if indeed it may be termed a principle, does not have universal validity.

Native churches may continue in need of financial aid for an indeterminate length of time. At present the churches of South Korea are a case in point. A church established in a leper colony would be another example.

In the apostolic age the self-government of gentile churches was not unrestricted. When Judaizers, by their insistence on circumcision for gentile converts to Christianity, created a serious problem for those churches, the matter was not left to their discretion but was referred to the Jerusalem Council, consisting of 'the apostles and elders', for decision (Acts 15). And, strange though it may seem, the church at Corinth needed to be told, and was told peremptorily by the apostle Paul, to excommunicate a member who was living in the sin of incest (I Cor. 5). Recent events in world history have proved that not every African tribe or nation is capable of civil self-government. The assumption that every native church is from the time of its founding capable of unaided self-government is hardly warranted.

No one would dare to say that the missionary Paul left it to the churches in the founding of which he had been instrumental, to educate themselves. Contrariwise, he kept educating them on his visits to them and by his epistles. In his second letter to the Corinthians, which was likely written in the year 57, some five years after his first visit to their city, he expressed the hope to preach the gospel in the regions beyond them 'when', said he, 'your faith is increased' (II Cor. 10:15, 16). Even from his Roman prison he laboured with might and main at the task of building up churches in the faith, and he kept doing so to the time of his execution.

In regard to self-propagation, as native evangelists address themselves to that necessary task, they may well in many instances find the missionary's advice and guidance invaluable.

Of late one often hears it said that churches consisting of recent converts should not be asked to adopt the historic creeds of Christendom but, instead, should be encouraged to work out their own versions of Christian doctrine.

Worse advice is difficult to imagine. It can be given only by such as are lacking in historical sense or else are hostile to the truth as it is in Christ. Is the Christian church of today to ignore practically the entire history of Christianity? Are there no lessons to be learned from the past? And are not such great confessions as, to name but a few, *The Nicene Creed*, *The Apostles' Creed*, *The Augsburg Confession*, *The Thirty-nine Articles of the Church of England*, *The Canons of Dort*, and *The Westminster Confession* products of the historic church's guidance into the truth by the Spirit of truth, promised to the church by its Head, even Jesus Christ (John 16:13)? To spurn that guidance is heinous sin.

16: God and Co-operation in Evangelism

Church and State

The old and thorny problem of the relationship of church and state arises frequently in the pursuit of evangelism. In foreign missions it has a way of becoming especially acute for the obvious reason that the missionary has to reckon with two governments, his own and that of the people among which he labours, and for the equally obvious reason that in many instances the latter government has not been influenced by Christian traditions.

What follows is not an attempt to say anything like the last word on this intricate problem. It is a brief statement of some theological principles bearing on the matter.

The position, occasionally taken, that the church because of its spiritual character must refuse to have dealings with the civil government is wholly untenable. It represents Anabaptism at its worst. The spiritual and the natural cannot thus be divorced. Both are divine creations, and the one God has revealed Himself in both. The natural serves as a necessary background for the spiritual. For instance, God first made the covenant of nature with Noah and in it guaranteed the continuity of the human race (Gen. 8:21, 22); subsequently God established with Abraham the covenant of grace, in which He guaranteed the continuity of the church (Gen. 17:7). The latter presupposed the former and even demanded it. And the state as well as the church is divinely instituted. 'Let every soul be subject unto the high powers. For there is no power but of God:

the powers that be are ordained of God' (Rom. 13:1).

Both preachers and politicians have been known to make the blunt statement that they believe in the 'absolute' separation of church and state. Such language is irresponsible. Those using it never made a serious attempt to think this matter through, for it is self-evident that no two areas of human life are completely independent of each other. When the state confronts a moral issue, as it often does, it becomes the church's duty to enlighten the state from the Word of God. If the state enacts a law which demands of its citizens violation of the moral law of God, who will deny that the church is in duty bound to protest? The state surely has something to say about the property rights of a church. And few, if indeed any, will care to deny that it is a God-assigned duty of the state to protect the church in the exercise of religious liberty.

Clearly, the proper relation of church and state is not a simple problem for every angle of which there is an easy solution. Yet, certain conclusions as to the bearing of this problem on evangelism would seem to be unassailable.

Let not the state engage in evangelism. It is a task assigned unmistakably by God to the church. The proper function of the state is quite another; namely, the punishment of evil-doers and the praise of those that do good (Rom. 13:3, 4); in short, the maintenance of justice in human relations. Here the principle of so-called sphere sovereignty applies. Strictly speaking, God alone has sovereignty. But the sovereign God has assigned authority – a relative sovereignty, if that be not a contradiction in terms – to the church and to the state in each of two areas of human life. As the church may not impinge on the sovereignty of the state, so the state may not impinge on sovereignty of the church. When King Saul, before joining battle with the Philistines, usurped the priestly function of bringing sacrifice to God, God rejected him as king over Israel (I Sam. 13:1-14). When King Uzziah presumed to burn incense in the temple, which was a prerogative of the priests as representatives of the church of the old dispensation, God smote him with leprosy (II Chron. 26:16-21). And when Charlemagne, founder of the Holy Roman Empire, forced entire nations at the point of the sword to receive Christian baptism, he went far beyond the limits which God has ordained for the civil government.

Let not the church ask the state for permission to preach the Word of God. To do so would constitute an ignominious surrender by the church of its God-given sovereignty, an outrageous substitution of the state for Christ as head of the church, an unpardonable recognition of state totalitarianism. Attention must here be called to as prevalent and pestilent a heresy as exists today. It is that men possess by the grace of the state such basic liberties as that of speech, that of assembly, that of the press, that of religion and worship. Such is not at all the case. These are *God-given* liberties and therefore *inalienable*. It was God also who bestowed upon the church the right as well as the duty to proclaim the gospel to the utmost bounds of the earth. Having received that right from the King of kings, the church may not supplicate the civil magistrate for it.

Let not the church permit itself to be degraded so as to become a tool of the state. All too often that has occurred in the past, notably in the post-Reformation period. By way of reaction from Rome, which taught the supremacy of the church over the state, the churches of the Reformation, by and large, went to the opposite extreme of Erastianism, which regarded the church as a phase of the state and therefore placed the church under state domination.

That accounts for the established or state churches of many European lands. It was not until the nineteenth century that free churches began to flourish, and to the present day they have by no means supplanted all established churches. Serious damage to the cause of Christian missions resulted. The fortunes of missions came to be bound up with the manoeuvring of European states in foreign politics. Briefly, foreign missions became to a considerable extent political. As striking and sad an example as any is afforded by the so-called Boxer uprising in the year 1900 in China. Due to the intervention of other governments in the internal affairs of that nation a wave of intense hatred against foreigners swept over the northern Chinese provinces, and numerous missionaries were slain.

It is a duty of the state to protect its citizens, the church included, in the exercise of religious liberty. On that proposition there is almost complete unanimity in present-day Protestantism. In its original form *The Westminster Confession of Faith*, being a product of the Reformation period, was marred by a strong Erastian note in its teaching of the relation of church and state to each other. In 1788, due in part, no doubt, to the influence of that great American Baptist, Roger Williams, American Presbyterians removed that error from this doctrinal standard. No longer did they assign to the civil magistrate the duty 'to take order, that unity and peace be preserved in the church, that the truth of God be kept pure and entire, that all blasphemies and heresies be suppressed, all corruptions and abuses in worship and discipline prevented or reformed, and all the ordinances of God duly settled, administered, and observed'. Nor did they continue to say: 'For the better effecting whereof, he hath power to call synods, to be present at them, and to provide that whatsoever is transacted in them be according to the mind of God'. Yet, significantly they insisted: 'As nursing fathers, it is the duty of civil magistrates to protect the church of our common Lord, without giving the preference to any denomination of Christians above the rest, in such a manner that all ecclesiastical persons whatever shall enjoy the full, free, and unquestioned liberty of discharging every part of their sacred functions, without violence or danger' (*The Westminster Confession of Faith*, XXIII, 3).

That this position is Scriptural permits of no doubt. It is implicit in the assertion concerning the magistrate, 'He is the minister of God to thee for good' (Rom. 13:4). Clearly to the point is the use made by Paul as missionary of his Roman citizenship. By virtue of that citizenship he could carry the gospel freely to all parts of the empire, and on at least three occasions when he suffered violence and injustice he insisted on that right. When the magistrates of Philippi ordered him and Silas released from prison, Paul protested vigorously: 'They have beaten us openly uncondemned, being Romans, and have cast us into prison; and now do they thrust us out privily? Nay verily; but let them come themselves and fetch us out' (Acts 16:37). When the Roman garrison at Jerusalem had taken Paul into protective custody and the chief captain gave orders that he should be examined by scourging, Paul said to the centurion standing by: 'Is it lawful for you to scourge a man that is a Roman, and uncondemned?' On being informed that his prisoner was a Roman, the chief captain was afraid and forthwith put a stop to Paul's examination (Acts 22:24–29). And when Porcius Festus, procurator of Judea, wishing to please Paul's Jewish persecutors, suggested that he be tried at Jerusalem rather than at Caesarea, the apostle rejected that injudicious proposal and made use of his privilege as a Roman citizen to appeal to the emperor (Acts 25 : 11). In the providence of the all-wise God that appeal resulted in the triumphant entry of the gospel into the capital city of the world.

Paul's writings contain a passage which bears most directly on the point at issue. It is I Timothy 2 : 1–4. The apostle exhorts that 'first of all, supplications, prayers, intercessions, and giving of thanks be made for all men : for kings and for all that are in authority'. He asserts that such prayers by Christians will be conducive to their leading 'a quiet and peaceable life in all godliness and honesty'. But he does not stop there. He goes on to say that God is pleased with the intercession of His people for their rulers and their consequent peaceable living, because these contribute to the accomplishment of God's desire, 'who will have all men to be saved, and to come unto the knowledge of the truth'. In fine, one teaching of this passage is that, if the civil magistrates govern as they should, that will enhance the spread of the gospel.

The fact having been established that it is a God-assigned function of the state to protect the church and its members in the pursuit of evangelism, some concrete conclusions are in order.

According to international law each nation is its own judge as to who may enter its domain and who is to be excluded. Therefore, although a church of Christ may never petition an earthly government for permission as such to preach the gospel, it is perfectly proper for a church to request a foreign government to admit a specific missionary, and it is just as proper for a church to enlist the aid of the homeland government in this procedure.

The missionary in a foreign land must show due respect for the rulers of that land, even if they are pagans. Likely

Paul wrote both his epistle to the Romans and his first letter to Timothy during the reign of infamous Nero. The divine command, 'Fear God. Honour the king' (I Peter 2:17) holds for evangelists as well as for others. And, wherever he may labour, in every legitimate way the evangelist must cultivate the good will of the civil magistrate.

It may not be wise in every instance for a foreign missionary to rely on protection by his own government. Some years ago an American missionary in China caused injury accidentally to a Chinese child. He was placed under arrest. According to 'extra-territorial rights' then in force, he might have insisted on being tried by an American court. Instead, he chose trial in a Chinese court and by so doing created much good will.

Well may the evangelist co-operate with civil authorities in the suppression of such social evils as slavery, prostitution, and the illegal sale of narcotics. However, when doing so he must distinguish between the function of the state and that of the church. The state combats such evils with 'the sword' (Rom. 13:4); the church combats them with 'the sword of the Spirit, which is the word of God' (Eph. 6:17).

Christianity and Other Religions

A view widely prevalent today is that Christianity is but one of the many religions of the world, in a class with all the others, although perhaps at the head of the class. From that premise the conclusion is drawn that the task of the Christian missionary is not to induce the adherents of another religion to replace it with Christianity, but rather to collaborate with men of other religions in a search for truth and goodness. In recent decades William Ernest Hocking of Harvard University, chairman of the commission which in 1932 produced *Rethinking Missions* and author of *Living Religions and a World Faith*, a 1940 publication, has been one of the foremost advocates of that view.

That the teaching of Holy Scripture is quite otherwise has already been pointed out. Although all the religions of humanity contain elements of truth, yet Christianity is the only true religion. The God of the Bible, who is the God of Christianity, is God alone (Ps. 86:10). All other gods are idols. Jesus Christ, the Christian Saviour, is the one Saviour (John 14:6; Acts 4:12). There is no other. Salvation by grace, which is the Christian way of salvation, is the only way (Eph. 2:8). Salvation by human effort, which is recommended by all other religions, can only end in destruction. Christian heterosoterism; that is, salvation by another, namely God, rules out autosoterism; that is, salvation by self.

Such, in summary, being the unmistakable teaching of God's infallible Word, the conclusion is inescapable that in evangelism co-operation of Christians with the adherents of other religions is to be rejected uncompromisingly.

Does it follow that no co-operation whatever is possible between Christians and, for example, Buddhists, Confucianists, Taoists, Shintoists, and Mohammedans? The answer to that question must be negative. Due to the common grace of God they can work together for such ends, to name but a few of many, as the reduction of illiteracy, social justice, and the conquest of disease. It is even conceivable that they might stand shoulder to shoulder in resisting the efforts of a totalitarian despot to deprive them of religious liberty. But, when it comes to evangelism,

[206]

they have no common message to proclaim. Here applies the absolutist injunction which the Apostle Paul addressed to those members of the Corinthian church who had not broken summarily with every practice of pagan worship: 'Be ye not unequally yoked together with unbelievers: for what fellowship hath righteousness with unrighteousness? and what communion hath light with darkness? and what concord hath Christ with Belial? or what part hath he that believeth with an infidel? and what agreement hath the temple of God with idols? For ye are the temple of the living God; as God hath said, I will dwell in them, and walk in them; and I will be their God, and they shall be my people. Wherefore come out from among them and be ye separate, saith the Lord, and touch not the unclean thing; and I will receive you, and will be a Father unto you, and ye shall be my sons and daughters, saith the Lord Almighty' (II Cor. 6:14–18).

Many students of religion are wont to say that Judaism and Christianity have one origin, that, since both honour the Old Testament as a sacred book, the religious messages which they proclaim cannot but have much in common, and that, therefore, they ought by all means to merge their efforts toward the evangelization of the world. That argumentation ignores the crucial fact that Judaism has rejected Jesus of Nazareth as the Messiah. And it is that fact which renders Judaism a false religion. Christ being the fullest revelation of Him who is the God of the Old and the New Testament alike, Judaism has turned its back on the only true God. It has spurned the one Saviour of mankind. It teaches reliance for salvation on the righteousness of man. Co-operation of Christianity with Judaism in evangelism is unthinkable.

Orthodoxy and Heterodoxy

Whether Protestantism and Roman Catholicism can collaborate in evangelism is little more than an academic question. Hitherto Rome has ruled out such collaboration and has even opposed Protestant evangelism vigorously. Today there are a few straws in the wind suggesting that the time may be at hand when that question will become actual. If and when that occurs, Protestantism will have to settle the issue whether Rome is to be regarded as a true church or a false. Calvin's boldly, yet carefully, worded appraisal of Rome may here be quoted: 'While we are unwilling simply to concede the name of Church to the Papists, we do not deny that there are churches among them. . . . I call them churches, inasmuch as the Lord there wondrously preserves some remains of His people, though miserably torn and scattered, and inasmuch as some symbols of the Church still remain – symbols especially whose efficacy neither the craft of the devil nor human depravity can destroy. But as, on the other hand, those marks to which we ought especially to have respect in this discussion are effaced, I say that the whole body, as well as every single assembly, wants the form of a legitimate Church' (*Institutes of the Christian Religion*, IV, II, 12). Protestantism will also have to face squarely the fact that many Roman teachings are anti-Christian, notably the doctrine of the meritoriousness of good works and that of sacerdotalism; namely, that the church not merely *proclaims* the grace of God, but actually *imparts* saving grace to men through the sacraments. A church which holds, as every Protestant church must, that the sinner is saved by the grace of God imparted to him by the Holy Spirit without the mediation of the church and that the merits of

Christ are the sole ground of salvation cannot possibly co-operate in evangelism with a church which insists on such heresies as the aforenamed. The present strong trend in the Church of Rome toward the exaltation of Mary to saviourhood likewise rules out collaboration.

Inexpressibly sad to say, a considerable segment of present-day Protestantism has become guilty of heresies worse than those of Rome. Although denying the sufficiency of the Bible as the Word of God, Rome upholds its infallibility; modernism denies Scriptural infallibility and brands the teaching of Scriptural inerrancy as harmful. Rome proclaims the essential and eternal deity of Christ; modernism rejects it. Rome teaches salvation by human merit in addition to the merits of Christ; modernism boldly asserts that salvation is by human merit alone. While Rome errs as to miraculous healing today, it rightly maintains Christianity as a supernatural religion; modernism rudely strips Christianity of its supernaturalism. Rome sets great store by the sacrificial death of the Son of God; modernism scorns a God who demands a bloody sacrifice for sin, particularly the bloody sacrifice of His own Son. J. Gresham Machen's *Christianity and Liberalism* first came from the press in 1924. It contended that the modernism of that day was not historic Christianity, but another religion. Obviously Machen was right. It is nothing strange that he was never confuted.

Let no one be so naïve as to think that the older modernism has had its day and is now defunct. It is extremely vocal still. But alongside of it has sprung up a new modernism which, while critical of the old, subscribes to its basic presupposition that the Bible, far from being the infallible and inerrant Word of God, is marred by numerous errors. Although it would be known as 'the new orthodoxy', it is neither a consistent repudiation of the older modernism nor anything like a wholehearted return to the doctrines of the Protestant Reformation. The fact that there exists a considerable variety of theological opinion within 'neo-orthodoxy' makes its evaluation difficult; but a few samples will reveal something of the vast gulf that yawns between the historic Christian gospel and the gospel according to this dialectical school of thought. Rudolf Bultmann insists that the gospel story as told by the four New Testament evangelists is in great need of being demythologized. Paul Tillich regards Jesus of Nazareth, not as the eternal Son of God, of the same substance with the Father, but as a human being who became divine. Karl Barth conceives of the reconciliation of God and man not so much as the satisfaction of the divine penal justice by Christ's self-sacrifice on the cross, but rather as a bridging of the chasm between God, the Creator, and man, the creature, which was effected when the Word became flesh; that is to say, by the incarnation. Barth also, to put it mildly, comes danger-ously near to teaching universal salvation.

It is a matter of common knowledge that both the old and the new modernism are extremely influential in the National Council of the Churches of Christ in the United States of America and the World Council of Churches. The high-sounding confessions of these councils of 'Jesus Christ as Divine Lord and Saviour' and 'our Lord Jesus Christ as God and Saviour' are left open to a wide range of interpretation. John Knox of Union Theological Seminary of New York regards the allegation that Jesus is God as a mere symbol.

In evangelism the co-operation of evangelicals with deniers of the cardinal teachings of the Christian religion is ruled out. It is forbidden, not only by the Apostle Paul's

anathematization of the preacher of a false gospel (Gal.
1 : 8, 9), but also by the Apostle John's injunction, 'If there
come any unto you, and bring not this doctrine, receive
him not into your house, neither bid him God speed' (II
John 10). To be sure, not all intercourse of believers and
unbelievers is to be avoided, for then believers would have
to go out of the world (I Cor. 5 : 10); but, as Meyer's *Commentary on the New Testament* has it, 'Not merely the
hospitable reception into the house, but also the friendly
greeting of the false teacher, if he comes as a Christian
brother, is not to take place.' In this age of 'religious
tolerance' the Christian church needs to be reminded of
this exclusivism prescribed by the apostle of love.

Evangelicals and Evangelicals

An evangelical may be defined as one who upholds the
fundamental teachings of historic Christianity. Implicit in
that definition is the *possibility* of collaboration of evangelicals in evangelism. The *need* of collaboration may also
be inferred, for what is more obvious than that those who
proclaim one gospel ought to present a united front in so
doing? The old saying, 'In unity there is strength' contains
at least a modicum of truth. From a human viewpoint it
would seem reasonable to expect that the impact of the
gospel will be strengthened by the unity of those who
declare it.

However, the *extent* of that co-operation presents problems which require study.

Ought all evangelical churches to unite in one world-
wide council of churches and assign the evangelization of
the world to that council? Concretely put, should such
organizations as the National Association of Evangelicals,

the World Evangelical Fellowship, the American Council of Christian Churches, and the International Council of Christian Churches merge and take over from the constituent denominations the task of world evangelism? Regrettable though it is that councils of evangelical churches are at present competing with each other, serious objections can be raised to that type of co-operation. To single out one, the aforenamed arrangement would in effect create a super-church. Yet, in reality a council of churches is not itself a church. But God has committed the proclamation of the evangel specifically to his *church*.

If each evangelical denomination regarded itself as the one true church of Jesus Christ, it would, as a matter of course, aim to reproduce itself on the mission fields of the world. But that is not at all the case. In spite of differences obtaining among them, evangelical churches, generally speaking, recognize one another as true churches. Yet, this does not mean that they are willing to relegate every difference to the limbo of the insignificant. For one example, a church which practices infant baptism from conviction, and not merely by force of tradition, will insist that the children of believers not only *may* but *must* be baptized by virtue of their inclusion in the covenant of grace. A Baptist church, on the other hand, will as a matter of principle baptize only adult believers. This difference cannot but have a bearing on evangelism. The paedobaptist evangelist will baptize the infant children of converts, the antipaedobaptist evangelist will not. And so a measure of denominationalism may be expected to persist on mission fields, even among evangelicals.

Obviously, all evangelical churches can co-operate in such evangelistic activities as, to name a few, translation of the Bible into various languages, distribution of the Word of God, making representations to the civil authorities in order to facilitate the admission of missionaries into foreign lands, the taking of whatever measures are proper and necessary to keep the airlanes open to orthodox religious broadcasts. In such matters they should work hand in hand. Churches honouring one another as true manifestations of the body of Christ ought also to practise a measure of what has come to be known as 'church comity'. In this context that means that they should show respect for one another's evangelistic efforts by ordinarily abstaining from interference with them. More positively, mutual helpfulness is often a desideratum.

The most serious obstacle to unrestricted co-operation among evangelicals remains to be considered. There are among them certain doctrinal differences which affect in a direct way the presentation of the gospel and are by no means insignificant. Here the difference between the Reformed faith and the faith of the Arminian must be named. They agree fully that the divine offer of salvation is perfectly sincere in the case of all to whom it comes and that nothing would please God more than the acceptance of that offer by all in faith. They also agree that the sinner is obligated to believe in Christ and that, in case he fails to meet that obligation, he will perish through his own fault, and not through any fault on the part of God. Yet there are appreciable differences. The Arminian will tell each sinner that God designed by the death of His Son to save him; the Calvinist will insist that Paul never once addressed a sinner thus, and that he could not have done it because this would have implied that mere man could thwart the plan of the Almighty. The Arminian will tell unregenerate man that he has the ability to believe in Christ and that, if he exercises that ability of his own free volition, he will be born again; the Calvinist will insist that unregenerate man, dead in trespasses and sins as he is (Eph. 2:1), will not and cannot come to Christ in faith except God draw him by the irresistible regenerating grace of the Holy Spirit (John 6:44). Let no one term these differences minor or ridicule them as mere hair-splitting. On this matter Benjamin B. Warfield says in *The Plan of Salvation*: 'The issue is indeed a fundamental one, and it is closely drawn. Is it God the Lord that saves us, or is it we ourselves? And does God the Lord save us, or does he merely open the way to salvation, and leave it, according to our choice, to walk in it or not? The parting of the ways is the old parting of the ways between Christianity and autosoterism' (p. 108).

And yet, grave though the issue is, there is cause for cheer. In their prayers Arminian evangelists frequently confess man's utter and complete dependence on God for conversion. And Arminians, too, have been known to sing:

> I sought the Lord, and afterward I knew
> He moved my soul to seek Him, seeking me;
> It was not I that found, O Saviour true;
> No, I was found of Thee.

God be thanked, there are numerous evangelicals, spread over many denominations, who find themselves in full agreement with one another on the gospel of Jesus Christ. Let them collaborate with wholehearted zeal in the spread of the good tidings of the grace of God.

17: God and the Effectiveness
of Evangelism

Communication of the Evangel

Of late a new science has come into being, or, more pre-cisely, an old science has been renamed. What long ago was termed rhetoric, subsequently elocution, and more re-cently public speaking, has come to be subsumed under *communication*. It is the science of conveying a message, whether by the spoken word, in writing, or by acting.

How much such evangelistic preachers as Wesley, Whitefield, Edwards, Spurgeon, Moody, Sunday, and Walter A. Meyer knew of communication as a science is difficult to say, but certain it is that they were masters of the art. That is true also of Evangelist Billy Graham and of Peter H. Eldersveld of the Back-to-God Hour, the radio broadcast of the Christian Reformed Church. Perhaps communication is primarily a gift, secondarily an art, and in a more remote sense also a science.

Occasionally one hears the Apostle Paul lauded as a great orator, even as the greatest orator the Christian church has ever had. There is good reason to doubt that he was so regarded in his day. In fact, it is practically certain that by the standards of the Graeco-Roman world he did not qualify as an orator at all. In sophisticated Corinth there were those who said of him: 'His letters are weighty and strong; but his bodily presence is weak and his speech of no account' (II Cor. 10:10 ASV). He himself told the Corinthians that he came to them 'not with excellency of speech' nor 'with enticing words of man's wisdom' but was with them 'in weakness and in fear and in much trembling' (I Cor. 2 : 1–4). He even admitted that he was 'unskilled in speaking' (II Cor. 11 : 6 RSV). Evidently Paul was neither a Demosthenes nor a Cicero. Yet, the impact which he made on his hearers is proof that he knew how to grip and hold an audience.

Communication is a matter of personality rather than technique. If a speaker has a certain type of personality, he is sure to command the attention of his audience without resorting to clever devices. If, on the other hand, he lacks a certain type of personality, the most cunning devices will not suffice to gain him a hearing. That being the case, the personality of the evangelist is of substantial importance.

Scripture takes cognizance of that fact when it teaches that ordinarily salvation is accomplished through the *preaching* of the Word of God. No doubt, sinners may be saved, and often are, by the mere reading of the Word, but as a general rule God is pleased to employ preaching to that end. The Ethiopian treasurer did not come to faith by his reading of Isaiah 53 but through Philip's *preaching* on that text (Acts 8 : 26–39). Referring to both Jews and Greeks, Paul put the rhetorical question: 'How shall they believe in him of whom they have not heard, and how shall they hear without a *preacher*?' (Rom. 10 : 14). The same preacher declared: 'The *preaching* of the cross is to them that perish foolishness; but unto us which are saved it is the power of God', and 'After that in the wisdom of God the world by wisdom knew not God, it pleased God by the foolishness of *preaching* to save them that believe' (I Cor. 1 : 18, 21). Now in preaching the personality of the preacher cannot but play a prominent part. To that fact Phillips Brooks gave expression in his otherwise in many respects defective definition of preaching as 'the communication of truth by man to men'.

What sort of person must the evangelist be in order to command the attention of his audience to the gospel? Some requisites are obvious. He must have a clear understanding of the gospel for the simple reason that vagueness and confusion can neither convey truth nor command respect. He must have a strong conviction as to the truth of the gospel so that he can say: 'I believe, and therefore have I spoken' (II Cor. 4:13) and 'I delivered unto you first of all that which I also received, how that Christ died for our sins according to the scriptures; and that he was buried, and that he rose again the third day according to the scriptures' (I Cor. 15:3, 4). He must have a lively sense of the supreme importance of the gospel, one's attitude to it being a matter of life or death, even eternal life or eternal death. He must himself have experienced the saving power of the gospel so that he can testify: 'I know whom I have believed, and am persuaded that he is able to keep that which I have committed unto him against that day' (II Tim. 1: 12). He must have a passion for lost souls which compels him to beseech them as though God were beseeching and to pray them in Christ's stead: 'Be ye reconciled to God' (II Cor. 5:20). He must have an overwhelming love for the Saviour, who first loved him, and therefore exclaim:

> Were the whole realm of nature mine,
> That were a present far too small;
> Love so amazing, so divine,
> Demands my soul, my life, my all.

Himself being a sinner saved by grace, he ought to proclaim the love of God more eloquently than can the angels.

Such communication of the evangel God is wont to bless and to use.

Bestowal of Conversion

The term *communication* is often given a more comprehensive sense than that in which it was employed in the foregoing discussion. Speakers, writers, and actors are said to communicate their *convictions* to those whom they address. Let it be said emphatically that communication in that sense far exceeds the power of the most eloquent and most godly evangelist. It is the task of the evangelist to communicate *the gospel* to men; to impart to man *faith in the gospel* is God's prerogative.

Saving faith is not a gift of the evangelist to his unsaved hearer; 'it is the gift of God' (Eph. 2:8). No evangelist ever imparted faith in Christ to a single soul; it is wrought in human hearts by the Holy Spirit, for 'no man can say that Jesus is the Lord, but by the Holy Ghost' (I Cor. 12:3). No sinner was ever converted by an evangelist; the author of conversion is God. Scripture accounts for Lydia's conversion, not by saying that she lifted the latch of her heart from within, nor yet by relating that the great apostle by his convincing reasoning and eloquent appeal softened her heart, but by insisting that the Lord opened her heart so that she attended to the things which were spoken of Paul (Acts 16:14).

It was in the full realization of the evangelist's complete dependence on God for the effectiveness of his labours that the church's most celebrated missionary wrote: 'Who then is Paul, and who is Apollos, but ministers by whom ye believed, even as the Lord gave to every man? I have planted, Apollos watered; but God gave the increase. So then neither is he that planteth any thing, neither he that watereth; but God that giveth the increase' (I Cor. 3:5–7).

It is the profound teaching of Holy Scripture that the ultimate explanation for a given person's coming to faith lies in God's sovereign election of him from the foundation of the world unto salvation. In the saying of Jesus, 'Many are called, but few are chosen' (Matt. 22:14), it is plainly implicit that of the many who are called by the gospel the few who believe do so because they were divinely chosen to that end from eternity. And Luke said in so many words that in response to the preaching of Paul and Barnabas to the gentiles at Antioch in Pisidia, 'as many as were ordained to eternal life believed' (Acts 13: 48). God did the ordaining. God also made good His ordaining by the imparting of saving faith.

On a London street a reeling drunkard collided with Spurgeon. He recognized the preacher and asked whether the preacher did not recognize him. When Spurgeon answered in the negative, the inebriate argued: 'But you ought to know me; I'm one of your converts.' To which came the apt reply: 'Right you may well be. If you were God's convert, you wouldn't be in your present condition.'

Condemned stands the advice often given to those who declare the gospel: 'Preach as if everything depended on you; pray as if everything depended on God.' He who preaches as if everything depended on himself proceeds on a false assumption. That cannot be good. He who prays as if everything depended on God declares a true assumption false. That is no better. Commendable, on the other hand, is the advice of William Carey, Baptist missionary to India: 'Except great things from God. Attempt great things for God.' The evangelist must indeed labour with all his might, but in complete dependence for results on the Holy Spirit. If he does that, his dependence cannot but come to expression in fervent prayer. And here, too, 'the prayer of a righteous man has great power in its effects' (James 5 : 16 RSV).

In many instances the evangelist presents the gospel to spiritually dead sinners. That the dead cannot raise themselves goes without saying. That no mere man can bring the dead to life likewise goes without saying. Only He is able to do that who, in one of Ezekiel's visions, spoke to the dry bones of the valley: 'Behold, I will cause breath to enter into you, and ye shall live: and I will lay sinews upon you, and will bring flesh upon you, and cover you with skin, and put breath in you, and ye shall live; and ye shall know that I am the Lord' (Ezek. 37 : 5, 6). Otherwise expressed, unbelief is a matter of the heart, the inmost disposition of one's being. The unsaved person has a heart of stone. He himself cannot substitute for it a heart of flesh, and neither can the evangelist. To give him a new heart is the prerogative of God the Holy Spirit, of Him who promised His idolatrous people: 'I will give them one heart, and I will put a new spirit within you; and I will take the stony heart out of their flesh, and will give them a heart of flesh' (Ezek. 11 : 19). Only he who has undergone that radical change of heart which Scripture terms the new birth will embrace the gospel in faith. For 'the natural man receiveth not the things of the Spirit of God; for they are foolishness unto him; neither can he know them, because they are spiritually discerned' (I Cor. 2 : 14).

From the truth that the effectiveness of evangelism depends wholly on God an unavoidable conclusion follows. It is that to God belongs all the glory for every genuine conversion. Let no convert take credit for his conversion. Let no evangelist take any credit for the conversion of him to whom he brought the gospel. All boasting is excluded.

[220]

'He that glorieth, let him glory in the Lord' (I Cor. 1:31). Every true conversion is of God, through God, and unto God. To Him be glory for ever (Rom. 11:36).

At times the fruits of evangelism are not as evident as the evangelist wishes and prays they might be. It may seem to him that he is ploughing on rocks and that none of the seed he sows falls on good ground. Then discouragement may ensue. And yet, he who strives zealously to bring both his message and his methods into harmony with the Word of God never has cause for despair. Contrariwise, he may trust God for results.

Only God omniscient can accurately appraise the results of evangelism. Only He can count converts. When through mass evangelism many thousands come to profess faith in Christ, only He who searches the reins and hearts of men (Rev. 2:23) can judge how many of them possess true and abiding faith. And when Robert Morrison, the father of Protestant missions in China, after twenty-eight years of zealous missionary endeavour numbered but ten souls as his hire, only God knew in how many additional hearts His Spirit was about to begin, or even had begun, a good work.

God sees the things of tomorrow as if they had occurred yesterday. Therefore the Son of God could say: 'One soweth, and another reapeth' (John 4:37). When by the direction of divine providence someone left a tract at a certain house in England, God had it planned that Richard Baxter (1615–1691), having been converted through the reading of that tract, would write *The Saints' Everlasting Rest*; that Philip Doddridge (1702–1751), moved by the reading of that treatise, would write *The Rise and Progress of Religion in the Soul*; that William Wilberforce (1759–1833), under the spell of that work, would write his *Practical Christianity*; and that Thomas Chalmers (1780–1847), founder of the Free Church of Scotland, profoundly influenced by that book, would develop into one of the greatest preachers of all time, whose sermons were to be published two years after his death in twenty-five volumes. When, at the gate of Damascus, God turned Saul of Tarsus, He knew that through the labours of that one convert millions would be brought into the kingdom to the very end of time. And when His own Son, dying the death of a criminal, concluded His earthly mission in what appeared to be complete failure and ignominious defeat, God knew that, lifted up on the cross, He would draw unto Himself from every kindred and tribe and people and nation a throng which no man could number (John 12:32).

The Word of God abounds in exceeding great and precious promises for him who labours in the gospel. He is told: 'He that goeth forth and weepeth, bearing precious seed, shall doubtless come again with rejoicing, bringing his sheaves with him' (Ps. 126:6). God assures him: 'As the rain cometh down, and the snow from heaven, and returneth not thither, but watereth the earth, and maketh it bring forth and bud, that it may give seed to the sower and bread to the eater; so shall my word be that goeth forth out of my mouth: it shall not return unto me void, but it shall accomplish that which I please, and it shall prosper in the thing whereto I sent it' (Isa. 55:10, 11). He is admonished to be stedfast, unmovable, always abounding in the work of the Lord, forasmuch as he knows that his labour is not in vain in the Lord (I Cor. 15:58). Because God is faithful and His counsel will stand (Isa. 46:10), he may rest fully assured that as many as are ordained to eternal life will believe and be saved (Acts 13:48).

With God as leader there is no room for despair. There is room only for strong faith, firm hope, and ardent love.

[222]

18: God and Resistance to Evangelism

God and Satan

The history of the human race is one of conflict – conflict between the woman's seed and the serpent's seed (Gen. 3:15), the church and the world; conflict primarily between Christ and Antichrist, God and Satan.

Ever since the fall of man into sin Satan has done his utmost to arrest the spread of the evangel and to render the evangel ineffective in the case of those to whom it comes.

One of the profoundest mysteries of history is that God permits Satan to oppose Him vigorously or, for that matter, at all. That God is almighty permits of no doubt whatever. 'He doeth according to his will in the army of heaven, and among the inhabitants of the earth: and none can stay his hand, or say unto him, What doest thou?' (Dan. 4:35). It follows that Satan cannot so much as stir without God's permission. That God is all-wise is likewise indisputable. That in wisdom He often permits Satan to wreak what impresses us human beings as havoc upon His kingdom is a foregone conclusion. Yet, that fact presents us with inscrutable mystery. It behoves us to exclaim: 'O the depth of the riches both of the wisdom and knowledge of God! How unsearchable are his judgments, and his ways past finding out!' (Rom. 11:33).

Occasionally God gives us a glimpse of His power and wisdom in the overruling of Satan's works so that they contribute to the coming of God's kingdom. An obvious instance is provided by an experience of the early church.

The stoning of Stephen ushered in 'a great persecution against the church which was at Jerusalem; and they were all scattered abroad throughout the regions of Judea and Samaria, except the apostles'. But 'they that were scattered abroad went everywhere preaching the word' (Acts 8 : 1–4). Persecution proved to be a blessing in disguise, for it resulted in the spread of the gospel. That process was repeated so often in the subsequent history of the church that it gave rise to the maxim that the blood of martyrs is the seed of the church.

Incomparably the most significant instance of God's overruling the works of the devil unto the coming of His own glorious kingdom is afforded by the death of God's Son. Satan entered into Judas Iscariot and persuaded him to betray the Lord (Luke 22 : 3). Filled with satanic hatred to the point of bursting, the Jewish religious leaders demanded crucifixion for their rival. And who can deny that Pontius Pilate was under Satan's spell when, although convinced of Jesus' innocence, he surrendered Him to the will of His enemies? Thus was perpetrated the most enormous crime of all time, the official murder of Him who was at once the Son of God and the only perfect man that ever walked on earth. But God overruled it all unto the salvation of the world. In fact He had planned it all from eternity. The Lamb of God was 'slain from the foundation of the world' (Rev. 13 : 8).

Glimpses such as these teach us to trust the infinite power and wisdom of God when His ways with His archenemy far surpass our finite understanding.

God and Anti-Christian Rulers

Human government is both a blessing and a curse. It is

needed for the maintenance of justice in human relations. Without it sin would run wild, much wilder even than it does. Human government also constitutes punishment for sin. When in the garden of Eden man rebelled against God's perfect rule, God, by way of punishment, subjected him to the exceedingly imperfect rule of his sinful and foolish fellows. No doubt, toward the end of time the rule of men by man will prove one grand fiasco. Even now the signs of the times point clearly in that direction.

And so it is not strange that again and again in the course of history the gospel has been opposed by governments. What is remarkable is that frequently, not to say usually, those civil rulers who resisted the Christian evangel did so in the name of religion. A few examples may be cited.

The Jewish Sanhedrin forbade the apostles to preach Jesus (Acts 4:18). In doing so, it was motivated by religious zeal, in this instance zeal for Judaism. The history of the early church tells of numerous violent persecutions by the Roman emperors. Claiming divinity for themselves, they would not tolerate the worship of the Nazarene instead of Caesar. In 1194 Alfonso the Second of Spain issued an edict to the effect that all who in any way aided or protected the Waldenses, or even listened to them, should be punished by confiscation of property and persecuted for *lèse majesté*. This was done in pursuance of a papal ban. In the Reformation period Protestantism was outlawed by Roman Catholic governments. Think of the Spanish Inquisition and the massacre of Saint Batholomew in France. To come to the present century, the Japanese government demanded of its subjects that they pay homage in the Shinto shrines to the emperor as the direct descendant of the sun-goddess Amaterasu. What was required was an act at once of patriotism and of religion, the two being inseparable in Shintoism. For, pointedly put, Japan worshipped Japan.

Today, too, anti-Christian states are suppressing the gospel. It is being done by Communist Russia and its satellites and, it would seem, even more stringently by Communist China. Once more it is being done in the name of religion. Communism, for all its blatant avowal of atheism, is a religion. Henry Nelson Wieman and Walter Marshall Horton were right when in their large volume, *The Growth of Religion*, they thus classified Communism. It is an exceedingly fanatical religion.

In view of the aforesaid facts it is not difficult to sympathize with those who teach that God has temporarily abdicated, that for the present Satan is god, and that Christ will not reign until a coming millennium. And yet, how wrong they are! He who commanded the barbarians from the north to grind to dust the iron empire of Rome, who with the breath of His mouth destroyed the supposedly invincible Spanish armada, who sent Japan down to crushing defeat in the second world war, is God indeed. By faith we know that He who sits in the heavens laughs; He has the kings of earth in derision. He speaks to them in His wrath and vexes them in His sore displeasure. He declares: 'Yet have I set my king upon my holy hill of Zion.' He has given to Him the heathen for His inheritance and the uttermost parts of the earth for His possession (Ps. 2:4–8). And at times he who in faith observes the signs of the times actually discerns the divine laughter.

God and False Religions

Nineteen centuries have elapsed since Christ commanded His church to make disciples of all the nations. At present less than a third of the earth's population lays claim to the Christian name. According to the 1961 *World Almanac*, the total population of the globe is somewhat more than 2,800,000,000. If Roman Catholicism, Greek Orthodoxy, and Protestantism are added together, less than 900,000,000 rate as Christians. And God alone knows how many of these are Christians only in name. That leaves, in round numbers, 1,900,000,000 as adherents of false religions.

The foregoing statistics do not take into account the so-called cults. To name a few of them, in the United States there are approximately 176,000 Spiritualists, 260,000 Jehovah's Witnesses, and more than 1,600,000 Mormons. They, too, propound false religions.

Mention must here be made of the disconcerting fact that much of Protestantism, not only in the United States, but throughout the world, has capitulated to modernism. Admittedly, modernism is difficult to define. There are different types and degrees of it. But without hesitation the assertion may be made that a modernism which denies the supernatural inspiration of the Bible, the miracles of the Bible, notably Christ's virgin birth and His bodily resurrection, as actual historical events, the ontological Trinity, the eternal and essential deity of Christ, the satisfaction of divine justice by Christ's sacrificial and substitutionary death, the deity and personality of the Holy Spirit, supernatural regeneration by the Holy Spirit, and salvation by grace through faith instead of by human effort, is a religion other than Christianity. And, Christianity being the only true religion, such modernism must of necessity be counted a false religion.

What may not be overlooked in this context is that some

of the world's false religions are riding high. Missionaries from the far east say that it is experiencing a powerful revival of Buddhism. And exceedingly alarming is the spread of Mohammedanism. Not only are there more than twice as many Moslems in the world as Protestants, the two numbering about 429,000,000 and 213,000,000 respectively, but an Islamic wave of tidal proportions is rolling over large parts of Asia and Africa.

Again we are baffled. If God is God, how is it that to outward appearances Christianity, the only true religion, is so feeble and impotent, and the false religions are so strong and influential? In partial answer to that query one can point to such events as the conquest of pagan western Europe by early Christian missions and the defeat of Mohammedanism in the battle of Tours in 732. When Islam was threatening to overrun the whole of Europe, God spoke: 'Thus far and no farther.' Western Europe was saved for Christianity. The God who brought that to pass is living today. But the ultimate answer is that, whether or not shortsighted men see it, the fact is indubitable that the Lord God omnipotent reigns (Rev. 19:6). And He has assured His church: 'Behold, I have created the smith that bloweth the coals in the fire, and that bringeth forth an instrument for his work; and I have created the waster to destroy. No weapon that is formed against thee shall prosper; and every tongue that shall rise against thee in judgment thou shalt condemn' (Isa. 54:16, 17).

God and the Unbeliever

Another aspect of the mystery confronting us in this chapter remains to be considered. If God is able to save and is 'not willing that any should perish but that all should come to repentance' (II Peter 3:9), how is it that there are those who reject the gospel in unbelief and therefore perish everlastingly?

In a very real sense there is nothing strange about the fact that many men perish. 'All have sinned and come short of the glory of God' (Rom. 3:23). By nature all are 'dead in trespasses and sins' (Eph. 2:1). All are deserving of eternal death. That such men should perish is no wonder. It is a wonder of divine grace that of them any at all are saved. It is a manifestation of truly marvellous grace that out of the fallen human race God from eternity chose certain persons unto everlasting life and that in the course of time He imparts to those persons, dead as they are, spiritual life, by which they are enabled to receive Christ in faith and thus are saved.

The Bible teaches unmistakably that God did not choose or elect all sinners to everlasting life. The very words *choose* and *elect* preclude that thought. He sovereignly chose some and sovereignly passed others by. He graciously elected some to salvation, and He decreed justly to leave others to their deserts. 'Hath not the potter power over the clay, of the same lump to make one vessel unto honour, and another unto dishonour? What if God, willing to shew his wrath, and to make his power known, endured with much longsuffering the vessels of wrath fitted to destruction: and that he might make known the riches of his glory on the vessels of mercy, which he had afore prepared unto glory?' (Rom. 9:21–23).

In perfect harmony with Scripture *The Canons of Dort* teach: 'That some receive the gift of faith from God, and others do not receive it, proceeds from God's eternal decree. . . . According to which decree He graciously softens the hearts of the elect, however obstinate, and inclines them to believe; while He leaves the non-elect in His just judgment to their own wickedness and obduracy. And herein is especially displayed the profound, the merciful, and at the same time the righteous discrimination between men equally involved in ruin' (I, 6).

However, the sovereignty of God as expressed in the decree of reprobation detracts nothing from human responsibility. God does not force the reprobate into hell; they perish because they will not come to Christ that they might have life (John 5:40). God is not the author of unbelief in those who perish as He is the author of faith in those who are saved. As Judas Iscariot, who betrayed the Lord in accordance with 'the determinate counsel and foreknowledge of God' (Acts 2:23), had to bear the full responsibility for his evil deed and therefore went to 'his own place' (Acts 1:25), so the reprobate perish because of their own wilful unbelief. Let no one think it ever occurs that one of the non-elect wishes to come to Christ in faith but finds his way blocked by a divine decree. In every instance the reprobate loves death rather than life (Prov. 8:36).

That, too, the Dort divines grasped and therefore they said: 'It is not the fault of the gospel, nor of Christ offered therein, nor of God, who calls men by the gospel and confers upon them various gifts, that those who are called by the ministry of the Word refuse to come and be converted. The fault lies in themselves' (*The Canons of Dort*, III-IV, 9).

Let it be clearly understood and emphatically stated: when a sinner is saved, *all* the glory belongs to God; when a sinner is lost, the sinner must bear *all* the blame.

Here is mystery indeed. Let not mere man meddle with it. The paradox of the sovereignty of God displayed in the eternal decree of rejection, on the one hand, and, on the other hand, the full responsibility of the unbeliever for his unbelief must be permitted to stand without any attempt at mitigation. Paul faced that paradox when, having declared concerning God, 'Therefore hath he mercy on whom he will have mercy, and whom he will be hardeneth', he entertained the unbeliever's question, 'Why doth he yet find fault? For who hath resisted his will?' Did the apostle attempt a solution of the problem posed? He did nothing of the kind. He only reminded his questioner that he was man and that God is God. Said he: 'Nay but, O man, who art thou that repliest against God? Shall the thing formed say to him that formed it, Why hast thou made me thus?' (Rom. 9:18-20). What Paul did was to appeal to the sovereignty of God. In effect he told the unbeliever: 'Because God is sovereign, He has a perfect right to harden you. And for precisely the same reason, because God is sovereign, He has a perfect right to hold you responsible for your hardening your heart. In short, God is God.'

That has been termed the Pauline theodicy, and such it is. A strikingly similar theodicy is found in the discourses of the Son of God. Having upbraided the cities wherein most of His mighty works were done for their failure to repent, and having told them that in the day of judgment it would be more tolerable for Tyre and Sidon and Sodom than for them, He spoke: 'I thank thee, O Father, Lord of heaven and earth, because thou hast hid these things from the wise and prudent, and hast revealed them unto babes. Even so, Father, for so it seemed good in thy sight' (Matt. 11:20-26).

In his gospel the apostle of love confronted the paradox under consideration, and he, too, firmly refused to compromise either of its elements. When many of the Jews rejected Christ, John explained: 'They believed not on him, that the saying of Esaias the prophet might be fulfilled which he spake, Lord, who hath believed our report and to whom hath the arm of the Lord been revealed? Therefore they could not believe, because that Esaias said again, He hath blinded their eyes and hardened their heart; that they should not see with their eyes, nor understand with their heart, and be converted, and I should heal them. These things said Esaias, when he saw his glory, and spake of him' (John 12:37–41). Presently he upheld the full responsibility of these unbelievers for their unbelief by recording the words of Jesus: 'He that rejecteth me, and receiveth not my words, hath one that judgeth him: the word that I have spoken, the same shall judge him in the last day' (John 12:48).

That unto God is due all the glory for the salvation of sinners is the emphatic teaching of the entire Bible. Is God also glorified in the damnation of the reprobate? Without equating the glorification of God in these so widely diverse instances, one can answer that question only with an unequivocal affirmative. All that God decreed He decreed unto His glory. Every event in human history, which is but the unfolding of the divine plan of foreordination, somehow redounds to the glory of God. The very works of Satan God overrules unto His glory. As to the result of evangelism, the evangelist Paul said: 'We are unto God a sweet savour of Christ, in them that are saved, and in them that perish; to the one we are the savour of death unto death; and to the other the savour of life unto life' (II Cor. 2:15, 16). Calvin has commented: 'Here we have a remarkable passage, by which we are taught that, whatever may be the issue of our preaching, it is, notwithstanding, well-pleasing to God, if the gospel is preached, and our service will be acceptable to him; and also that it does not detract in any degree from the dignity of the gospel that it does not do good to all; for God is glorified even in this, that the gospel becomes an occasion of ruin to the wicked, nay, it must turn out so.' He has added: 'The gospel is preached for salvation: this is what properly belongs to it; but believers alone are partakers of that salvation. In the meantime its being an occasion of condemnation to unbelievers – that arises from their own fault.' Of the non-elect *The Westminster Confession of Faith* asserts: 'The rest of mankind, God was pleased, according to the unsearchable counsel of His will, whereby He extendeth or withholdeth mercy as He pleaseth, for the glory of His sovereign power over His creatures, to pass by, and to ordain them to dishonour and wrath for their sin, to the praise of His glorious justice' (III, 7).

God is sovereign. To detract from His sovereignty is to deny Him as God.

Man is a free and responsible agent. The unbeliever rejects Christ, not under external compulsion, but of his own choice; yet, under the compulsion of his own nature. His choice is determined by what he is – a totally depraved sinner, at enmity with God. 'The carnal mind is enmity against God: for it is not subject to the law of God, neither indeed can be' (Rom. 8:7).

19: God and the Triumph of Evangelism

Triumph Assured

The Psalmist sang: 'All the ends of the world shall remember and turn unto the Lord: and all the kindreds of the nations shall worship before thee' (Ps. 22:27). Another Messianic psalm foretold: 'He shall have dominion also from sea to sea, and from the river unto the ends of the earth: They that dwell in the wilderness shall bow before him; and his enemies shall lick the dust. The kings of Tarshish and of the isles shall bring presents; the kings of Sheba and Seba shall offer gifts. Yea, all kings shall fall down before him: all nations shall serve him' (Ps. 72:8–11). The stone which, in Nebuchadnezzar's dream, was cut out without hands and smote the image of iron, clay, brass, silver, and gold so that it resembled chaff of the summer threshing-floors 'became a great mountain and filled the whole earth' (Dan. 2:31–35). The day is coming when all things will be subdued unto the Christ (I Cor. 15:27, 28).

True it is beyond the shadow of a doubt that the Word of God teems with promises of coming triumph. But that is not all. Scripture describes the victory of God and Christ as present reality. That, in the conflict of the ages between God and Satan, God is ever in complete control hardly needs to be said. It is inherent in His being God. 'God reigneth over the heathen; God sitteth upon the throne of his holiness' (Ps. 47:8). 'The Lord is a great God and a great King above all gods' (Ps. 95:4). The mediatorial kingship of Christ, too, is even now glorious reality. The decisive battle between Christ and Satan was fought on

Calvary. It was there that Satan bruised Christ's heel but Christ bruised Satan's head (Gen. 3:15). Three times in the New Testament Satan is denominated 'the prince of this world', and each time it is said of him that as prince of the world he went down to defeat before the crucified Christ. With direct reference to His death on the cross Jesus said: 'Now is the judgment of this world: now shall the prince of this world be cast out' (John 12:31). With the shadow of the cross rapidly closing in on Him, He told His disciples: 'Hereafter I will not talk much with you; for the prince of this world cometh and hath nothing in me' (John 14:30). And, promising them the Holy Spirit to comfort them in their sorrow over His impending departure, He assured the disciples that the Spirit would reprove the world of judgment 'because the prince of this world is judged' (John 16:11. Whatever influence Satan has since exercised on the affairs of men – and it is admittedly great, so great that he is spoken of as 'the god of this world' who 'hath blinded the minds of them which believe not, lest the light of the glorious gospel of Christ, who is the image of God, should shine on them' (II Cor. 4:4) – he has exercised with Christ's permission and under His control. For Christ has indeed 'all power in heaven and in earth' (Matt. 28:18), and through His death He has destroyed him that had the power of death; that is, the devil (Heb. 2:14).

Here the question may be raised whether Scripture teaches that the future will bring spiritual blessings to the Israelitish people. Regrettably, there is no unanimity on that question among Bible-believers. On the one hand, there are those who hold that, while individual Jews may well from time to time turn to Christ, all the spiritual blessings promised in Scripture to the Jewish people have been inherited by spiritual Israel, which is the church. On the other hand, there are those who teach that on one day, the day of Christ's return, the Jewish nation in its entirety will experience a spiritual rebirth. Without wishing to be dogmatic, the writer would call attention to three statements of Scripture which he considers crucial as regards this problem. All are found in Romans 11. Paul puts the question, if the casting away of the Jews resulted in the reconciliation of the world, as it did, 'what shall the receiving of them be, but life from the dead?' (vs. 15). The apostle would seem to be envisaging a time when the Jewish people, who were rejected by God because they rejected His Son, will be received by God in mercy and will become instrumental in imparting a rich blessing to all of Christendom. The apostle continues: 'I would not, brethren, that ye should be ignorant of this mystery, lest ye should be wise in your own conceits; that blindness in part is happened to Israel, until the fulness of the gentiles be come in' (vs. 25). Are we not told here that spiritual blindness has affected Israel only in part, that this partial blindness is temporary, and that, when the full quota of the gentiles has been gathered into the church, God's ancient people will in large numbers receive the gospel? The conclusion is drawn: 'And so all Israel shall be saved' (vs. 26). Although several expositors of note are convinced that the term 'all Israel' refers to spiritual Israel, consisting of both Jewish and gentile believers, and other expositors are of the opinion that it designates the entire Jewish nation without any exception, there are good reasons for taking it to define the Jewish people as a whole, Jewry viewed collectively, although not distributively. F. L. Godet's discussion of this point in Appendix E of his *Commentary on Romans* is enlightening, and so is a booklet by William Hendriksen on this theme.

Triumph through Tribulation

What does the future have in store for the church of Christ? On that matter there is considerable difference of opinion among students of the Word of God.

Premillenarians generally teach that, although the gospel will be spread over the globe and many will turn to Christ, yet, by and large, the near future is dark for the cause of Christ. The time is coming, and may well be at hand, when Satan will have his way as well as his day. There will be great tribulation on earth. Either before or after the tribulation the saints will be raptured to meet Christ in the air. Christ will return in triumph and establish His millennial reign with Jerusalem as its centre. During that period Satan will be bound. At its close he will be loosed and will gather the nations from the four quarters of the earth against the beloved city. However, the devil will go down to defeat and, together with his allies, will be cast into the lake of fire and brimstone.

Postmillenarians so called are of two kinds. Many of them believe that the kingdom of God will come through such human efforts as social reform and that the completion of that process will constitute the reign of Christ. Those who hold that view base it upon an evolutionary view of history rather than upon the Word of God. But there are also supernaturalistic postmillenarians. They think it the teaching of Scripture that the preaching of the gospel will prove so effective that eventually all nations will turn to Christ, Christianity will be gloriously triumphant, a golden age will ensue, and that, when this has come to pass, Christ will return as Lord of all.

At this point a warning would seem to be in order. The differences between premillennialism and supernaturalistic postmillennialism, material though they are, may not be stressed so as to obscure the significant fact that both teach the ultimate and complete triumph of the Christ.

There obtains among those who accept the Bible as the Word of God a third view of things to come. It is known as amillennialism and would seem to be more comprehensively Scriptural than is either of the aforenamed views. That is to say, its proponents strive zealously, and not without success, to do justice to *all* the Scriptural data bearing on the subject in hand. In summary it is as follows. 'The thousand years' of Revelation 20 represent in symbolic language a long and complete period; namely, the period of history from Christ's ascension into heaven until His second coming. Throughout that age Christ reigns and the saints in glory reign with Him (vs. 4). Satan is bound in the sense of not being permitted to lead the pagan nations against Christendom (vss. 2, 3). In other words, in that period, which is the present, the so-called Christian nations are predominant in power and influence among the nations of the earth. During that period also takes place under the rule of Christ what may be termed the parallel development of the kingdom of light and that of darkness. This is unmistakably taught in Scripture. For example, Jesus' parables of the mustard seed and the leaven (Matt. 13:31-33) teach the growth of Christ's kingdom; and the growth of Satan's kingdom is patently implicit in the Saviour's plaintive query: 'When the Son of man cometh, shall he find faith on the earth?' (Luke 18:8). That two-fold process is being exemplified in current events. The heathen nations are slowly being Christianized, while the Christian nations are reverting to paganism. Toward the end of 'the thousand years' Satan will be loosed for a little while. Those will be dark days for the church of God.

Then will come to pass what is written in Revelation 13. Under the totalitarian rule of the Antichrist the human race will be consolidated politically, religiously, and economically. All men will follow him with the exception of those whose names are written in the book of life of the Lamb slain from the foundation of the world. The saints will suffer persecution. Satan will go forth to deceive the non-Christian nations in the four quarters of the earth, Gog and Magog, and gather them, numerous as the sand of the sea, to battle against the church and Christendom. The annihilation of Christ's kingdom will appear to be inevitable. However, fire will come down from God out of heaven and consume His foes. And the devil, together with his associates, will be consigned to eternal torment in the lake of fire and brimstone (Rev. 20:7–10). Christ will return in ineffable glory and, having raised the dead, will sit in judgment on all men (Rev. 20:12, 13).

Thus victory will be achieved through warfare, triumph through tribulation.

Triumph Consummated

Is one to conclude that, except for the conversion of a relatively small number of individuals, the proclamation of the evangel will prove of negligible effect and that, when the evangelization of the world by the church has resulted in failure, the Son of God will suddenly wrest victory from Satan by a cataclysmic display of power? Not by any manner of means.

The teaching of Scripture is plain. Toward the end of time Christ will indeed by a cataclysmic manifestation of power destroy His enemies. But it is also true that a countless throng from every kindred and tongue and people and nation will press through the twelve gates – three on the east, three on the north, three on the south, and three on the west – of the holy city, the new Jerusalem, come down from God out of heaven (Rev. 21:2, 13). The dwellers in that city, Abraham's spiritual seed, will be as numerous as the grains of sand on the seashore and as the stars in the black-blue firmament of night(Gen. 22:17). Together they will constitute the new and true humanity and as such will inhabit the new heaven and the new earth (Rev. 21:1). And that multitude will have been saved *through the gospel*.

Throughout the centuries men have striven to reunite divided humanity. One might almost say that those strivings constitute the history of mankind. Among the methods employed to accomplish that end three stand out. Countless attempts have been made to unite the nations by the sword. Thus came into being the world empires of ancient history as well as certain empires and dominions of medieval and modern times. Such strivings could only fail, for when men are united by force they are not united at all. Alexander the Great sought to hold together his worldwide domain by means of a universal language. He made Greek the language of literature the world over. The Church of Rome employs the same device when it seeks to hold its sons and daughters together by the common use of the Latin tongue. Volapuk and Esperanto are similar attempts of recent date to contribute to the unity of the race. It hardly needs to be said that the disease of disunity is too deep-seated to be healed by so feeble and superficial a remedy. Most recently men would heal humanity's breaches by such governmental organizations as the League of Nations, the World Court, and the United Nations. Who knows? By the common grace of God such organizations may possibly alleviate some of the world's woes. Conceivably they could head off or postpone a war or two. But certain it is that they, too, will fail miserably to establish universal peace.

Not one of the aforenamed devices of men, the last included, can bring about a united world. The reason is apparent. They deal only with symptoms, not with the cause, of humanity's disease. The cause is sin. Sin underlies disunity, strife, and war. And sin cannot be abolished by the sword, nor by oneness of language, nor yet by the assembled statesmen of the nations, men of good will though many of them are. Only God can conquer sin. His Son has done it. By His death on Calvary's cross He vanquished sin. That is the theme of the gospel. The Christian evangel is nothing else than the presentation of God's solution for the problem of sin. Only when it has been preached in the whole world and through it the nations have been made disciples of the Christ, will it come to pass that 'they shall beat their swords into ploughshares and their spears into pruninghooks: nation shall not lift up a sword against nation, neither shall they learn war any more' (Micah 4:3).

Christ's triumph, then, will be the triumph of evangelism. That is implicit, to say the very least, in the concluding words of the Great Commission: 'Lo, I am with you alway, even unto the end of the world' (Matt. 28:20). What else can this mean but that to the end of time He who has all power and authority on earth and in heaven will prosper His church in the proclamation of the evangel? Therefore it is written: 'They shall not hurt nor destroy in all my holy mountain; for the earth shall be full of the knowledge of the Lord as the waters cover the sea' (Isa. 11:9). Of the victors in the strife it is said that they overcame 'by the blood of the Lamb, and by the word of their testimony' (Rev. 12:11). And He who, riding upon a white horse, leads the armies of heaven to consummate triumph is named 'The Word of God' (Rev. 19:13).

Index of Scripture Passages